PLACE IN RETURN BOX to remove this checkout from your record.
TO AVOID FINES return on or before date due.
MAY BE RECALLED with earlier due date if requested.

GULL LAKE LIBRARY

DATE DUE	DATE DUE	DATE DUE

CONIFERS

SECOND EDITION

Trompenburg Arboretum

CONIFERS
SECOND EDITION

Text by

D. M. van Gelderen

Photographs by

J. R. P. van Hoey Smith

Translated from the Dutch language by

G. J. E. TenKate

Published in cooperation with
ROYAL BOSKOOP HORTICULTURAL SOCIETY
by
TIMBER PRESS

ISBN 0-88192-153-X

TIMBER PRESS, INC.
9999 S.W. Wilshire, Suite 124
Portland, Oregon 97225

Printed in Hong Kong

Contents

Photograph Locations

Foreword

I am most happy to comply with the request of the Royal Boskoop Horticultural Society to write a Foreword for this Jubilee book on conifers published on the occasion of the 125th anniversary of the Society.

A large number of conifers are described and beautifully illustrated in this new standard work. Many of the cultivars in the rich assortment of conifers have, in fact, been produced with the help of the Society. From its beginning, the Society set as one of its tasks the judging of new introductions into Dutch horticulture.

The development of a worthwhile and varied assortment of plants is another of the important objectives that the Society has set itself. And lastly, the publications of the Society have contributed enormously to the advancement of the expertise of its growers as well as others involved in the nursery trade.

Many developments have come about within the nursery trade in the past few years. For instance, the area under cultivation has increased significantly. Additionally, cultivation has intensified considerably through the introduction of new techniques—I'm thinking of pot and container culture, for example. New developments will surely be introduced in the coming years. Innovations in marketing, and movement in the direction of more centralized management and organization will mark the nursery sector. Despite these changes attention must be continually paid to quality and maintenance of a wide variety of plant material. In short, the future will impose important tasks on the Royal Boskoop Horticultural Society as well as the whole horticultural sector.

Living greenery will always fulfill an indispensable function in the maintenance of a livable environment. That is true the world over. The importance of the horticulture in the future cannot be over-emphasized.

Through the publication of this beautiful reference book, the literature of the ornamental horticulture has been truly enriched.

I would like to congratulate the Royal Boskoop Horticultural Society on this publication—to which the Rabobank has been pleased to lend her cooperation.

ir. P.J. Lardinois
Chairman, Board of Directors, Rabobank Nederland

Foreword

It is with the greatest pleasure that I comply with the request of the editors to write a Foreword to this book.

With this publication a tradition of the Royal Boskoop Horticultural Society, started in the last century, is continued.

In 1868, the *Nederlandsche Boomgaard (Dutch Orchard)* was published, a reference book unequaled for that time, in which the editors described hundreds of fruit varieties—apples, pears, cherries, plums, etc. The book contained numerous beautiful color pictures, quite unusual for a book of that time. 1200 copies were sold in a short time. The Dutch Royal Family even signed up for 6 copies.

In 1875, the *Nederlandsche Flora en Pomona (Dutch Flora and Pomona)* was published. The publication, with a printing of 1000 copies, was also sold out in a short time. As the title indicates, not only fruiting plants, but ornamental plants were described. This book maintained the same high standards of its predecessors and was published in almost the same format as the *Nederlandsche Boomgaard.*

Since that time our Society has launched many other publications. Space does not permit mentioning all of them. However, I want to make an exception for *Dendroflora,* since 1964 a yearly publication issued in cooperation with the Dutch Dendrology Society and printed in 3500 copies. In it, the work of our Judging Committee is summarized, including the judging of new cultivars, the results of varietal comparisons, the usefulness of various plants, etc.

This conifer book has come into being thanks to the cooperation of the following gentlemen:

J.R.P. van Hoey Smith (photographs)
D.M. van Gelderen (text)
W.M. van Nierop and
P.J. Stolwijk

The author is a true connoisseur of conifers. Mr. van Hoey Smith is director of the Arboretum 'Trompenburg' in Rotterdam.

This book is published on the occasion of the 125th anniversary of our Society which was founded in 1861 and received the designation "Royal" on its 100th anniversary in 1961. It now has approximately 800 members.

The reader will find over 1000 conifers illustrated in this book. Every genus is represented in proportion to its importance in horticulture.

The publication was made possible by the Head Office of the Rabobank in Utrecht/Holland, which not only backed us financially, but also gave us valuable advice.

I am happy to send this unique book off with my best wishes for the future.

Boskoop, January, 1986 Jan B.B. Tromp,
Chairman, Royal Boskoop
Horticultural Society

Acknowledgments

We wish to thank the following persons, who helped us greatly:

Prof. Dr. H.C.D. de Wit, Agricultural University, Wageningen, The Netherlands

Ir. B.C.M. van Elk, Research Station for Arboriculture, Boskoop, The Netherlands

Both gentlemen read the text and made corrections where necessary.

C.G. Bulk
H.J.J. van Gelderen-Esveld
K.A. Koemans
J.P. Kortmann
A.M. Vergeer

All professional nurserymen in Boskoop, their cooperation was most helpful in reviewing the many thousands of transparencies, from which those included were selected.

Dirk van Gelderen, secretary, also computerized the text.

Last, but not least, Mrs. van Hoey Smith, who received us with exceptional hospitality during the many sessions, all held in her home.

The book-committee,

J.R.P. van Hoey Smith
D.M. van Gelderen
W.M. van Nierop
P.J. Stolwijk

CONIFERS

Conifers are usually evergreen trees with branched stems, sometimes also shrubs, often with long shoots and short branches, as in *Cedrus* and *Larix*. The leaves are shaped, scale-like or needlelike; the needles are solitary or in bundles (*Pinus*). Sometimes the leaves have a distinct blade as in *Phyllocladus, Agathis.*

The male flowers are numerous and consist of a cone bearing pollen on the stamen. The female flowers consist of a cone with bract scales and seed scales from which the seed group. The ripe seeds are borne in cones or are nutlike or sometimes as coneberries. The number of seed lobes varies from 2 to 16.

There are 6 families of approximately 50 genera and about 500 species. Some species form expansive forests in the cold and temperate zones of the Northern Hemisphere.

The conifers all belong to the division GYMNO-SPERMAE. This division is divided into classes. For this book two classes are important; i.e., the class CONIFEROPSIDA, and the class TAXOPSIDA. The CONIFEROPSIDA contains all conifers, with the exception of the TAXACEAE which is the only family classified in the TAXOPSIDA. The CONIFEROP-SIDA consists of only one series, the CONIFERAE.

The series CONIFERAE includes 6 families: PINACEAE, TAXODIACEAE, CUPRESSACEAE, PODOCARPACEAE, CEPHALOTAXACEAE and ARAUCARIACEAE. These 6 families are subdivided in genera. The family name is given for each genus mentioned. Each genus contains a number of species. The valid species names are summed up at the end of the description of each genus without the names of the authors. To obtain the full botanical name, please refer to the botanic literature.

In this book the genera are fairly consistently described in the same order as they appear in the reference work of Dr. G. Krüssmann: *Manual of Cultivated Conifers,* 2nd Edition. In Krüssmann, the genera and species are comprehensively described in alphabetical order. In this book attention has been given to the characteristics of the genera. Consequently, in some genera, the species are not dealt with alphabetically because natural relationships and/or geographical origin are considered to be more important that retaining a strict alphabetical order. The genera *Ginkgo, Ephedra* and *Welwitschia* also belonging to the GYMNOSPERMAE are not discussed.

Abies/PINACEAE

The genus *Abies* contains about 50 species and well over 150 cultivars. A number of the species are not in cultivation. No cultivars are known of many species growing only in the wild. *Abies* is distributed over the whole of the Northern Hemisphere, with heavy concentrations in East Asia and North America. Some species are found in Europe and North Africa. All species are evergreen; they develop into large trees with a conical habit; the branches are radially arranged. The bark of mature trees is usually thick and rough. The leaves (usually needles) are commonly arranged in a pectinate form, although in several species the needles are arranged around the twig (*A. numidica, A. pinsapo*).

The underside of the needles is often silver-blue to light green. All *Abies* are monoecious, the male "flowers" are pendulous and solitary in short little racemes (clusters); the female inflorescence is upright and grows into an upright cone, that sometimes is quite large (*A. procera*). When the seeds are ripe, the cones completely disintegrate, the rachis remains, the seeds with their cover scales drop out. This characteristic distinguishes *Abies* and *Cedrus* from *Picea*. *Picea* species have permanent cones, that drop off intact. A characteristic of all *Abies* species is that, when one carefully pulls a needle from a twig no piece of the skin is torn off, which is always the case in *Picea*. In *Abies*, a round scar is left on the twig.

Linnaeus classified all *Abies* species known at that time under *Pinus*. This soon appeared to be untenable, so Miller split off *Abies* as a separate genus. In keeping with today's views, *Abies* is divided into two subgenera. All species except one, belong to the subgenus *Sapinus*. Only *A. bracteata*, with its sharp needles, is classified under the subgenus *Pseudotorreya*. The subgenus *Sapinus* is divided in 7 sections. The section *Nobilis* (1) contains two species, the very well-known *A. magnifica* and *A. procera*. The section *Diamel* (2) contains 4 species of which only *A. religiosa* is sometimes cultivated. The section *Balsamea* (3) is present in Northern and Central America and contains 9 species. Well-known representatives are *A. amabilis, A. balsamea, A. concolor, A. grandis,* and *A. lasiocarpa*. Next is the section *Pichta* (4) with 6 East-Asian species. Some well-known species are *A. koreana* and *A. veitchii*. The section *Momi* (5) contains 10 species that are subdivided into 3 subsections. To the section *Momi* belong among others *A. delavayi, A. firma,* and *A. homolepis*. Next comes the section *Peuce* (6) with 11, mainly European, species such as *A. alba, A. cephalonica,* and *A. nordmanniana*. Finally, the section *Pindrau* (7) with only 2 little known species: *A. pindrow* and *A. spectabilis.*

Abies cilicica. This handsome species is not often found in cultivation. It grows fast, but is susceptible to late frosts in April and May. The species is shown here in its natural habitat in the Taurus mountains in Turkey.

The species of *Abies* are not suited to smaller gardens, because they become too large. An exception is *A. koreana*, which grows modestly and can be very beautiful. One can find *Abies* as a rule only in arboreta and large parks. Some arboreta have important collections (Pinetum Bedgebury, Kent, Great Britain; Les Barres, Nogent-sur-Vernisson, France; Pinetum Blijdenstein, Hilversum, The Netherlands). Several of the well-known species have yielded a number of cultivars, that are far more satisfying as garden plants than the species.

From the European species, *A. alba*, some very beautiful cultivars have been developed. *A. alba* 'Pendula' is a contorted weeping form. *A. alba*

'Pyramidalis' is very useful in the smaller garden. From *A. amabilis* a broadly spreading form was developed at Pinetum Blijdenstein, Hilversum, Holland, with the name 'Spreading Star'.

A. balsamea 'Nana' is a very good dwarf form that also does well in rock gardens. An uncommon but highly recommended dwarf form is *A. cephalonica,* 'Meyers Dwarf'. The frequently cultivated *A. concolor,* which grows to more than 60 m in its native habitat, contains some rare dwarf forms, such as *A. concolor* 'Compacta' and 'Gable's Weeping'.

A. delavayi is one of the most beautiful species with very long dark green needles.

A. grandis (A. excelsior) is an imposing tree. Beautiful specimens can been seen in the Pinetum Schovenhorst, Putten, the Netherlands. It is a useful tree in forestry, especially along the Pacific Coast of North America.

A. koreana is perhaps the most beautiful *Abies* which is also suitable for use in smaller gardens. This species forms beautiful purplish blue cones when still immature, that turn brown when ripe. It is not uncommon for trees 60–70 cm high to bear cones. The cultivars of *A. koreana* are no more beautiful than the species. From the American *A. lasiocarpa* comes a very nice 'Compacta', often named *A. arizonica* 'Compacta', with silver-blue, densely packed needles.

A. nordmanniana comes from the Caucasus and becomes a beautiful tree. There is a weeping form 'Pendula' and a golden-yellow dwarf form 'Golden Spreader' which does not tolerate sun well.

A beautiful cultivar 'Glauca' from *A. numidica* has stiff, greenish blue needles around the twig. The Spanish fir *A. pinsapo* can never be confused with any other species because the blunt needles are arranged around the twig in a strictly radial pattern. The cultivar *A. pinsapo* 'Glauca' is very well known and widely grown. The best known species is *A. procera* which is often cultivated and sold under the name *A. nobilis*. The species comes from the west coast of the United States; the cultivar 'Glauca' is widely available. This cultivar forms large cones as a young tree, sometimes (to) 25 cm long with a diameter of 10 cm. In cultivation *A. veitchii* is often confused or mixed with *A. koreana*. *A. veitchii* is less beautiful but grows much faster than the typical *A. koreana*. Moreover the cones, which also develop on young trees, are usually green.

Several species are very important in commercial forestry. In Europe *A. alba* is widely planted for this purpose. In America, *A. concolor, A. grandis, A. lasiocarpa* and *A. procera* are planted on a large scale. In the coastal regions of western North America planting is hardly ever necessary, because of the enormous natural regeneration of the forests. Indeed, good forest management requires the removal of some young trees. In southwestern Europe *A. pinsapo* is sometimes planted for reforestation purposes. In southern Spain and northern Africa forests of *A.*

Abies lasiocarpa. One of the tallest trees along the west coast of North America. Pictured here in its habitat in Mt. Rainier National Park, USA.

3

marocana and *A. numidica* can be found. In southeastern Europe *A. cephalonica*, *A. cilicica* and *A. nordmanniana* are important forest species.

Abies is seldom found in northwestern Europe save in the coastal regions. *A. procera* is cultivated for the production of Christmas greens, particularly in Denmark.

In the framework of this photobook, detailed descriptions of the plants are omitted because the pictures speak for themselves. For detailed descriptions please refer to the literature.

A. alba	A. mariesii
A. amabilis	A. marocana
A. × arnoldiana	A. nebrodensis
A. balsamea	A. nephrolepis
A. borisii-regis	A. nordmanniana
A. bornmuelleriana	A. numidica
A. bracteata	A. oaxacana
A. cephalonica	A. pardei
A. chensiensis	A. pindrow
A. cilicica	A. pinsapo
A. concolor	A. procera
A. delavayi	A. recurvata
A. durangensis	A. religiosa
A. equi-trojani	A. rolii
A. fargesii	A. sachalinensis
A. firma	A. sibirica
A. fraseri	A. spectabilis
A. grandis	A. squamata
A. guatemalensis	A. sutchuenensis
A. hickeli	A. tacanensis
A. holophylla	A. × vasconcellosiana
A. homolepis	A. veitchii
A. × insignis	A. vejari
A. kawakamii	A. × vilmorinii
A. koreana	A. yuana
A. magnifica	

Acmopyle/PODOCARPACEAE

This is a small genus, split off from *Podocarpus*, and native to the Fiji Islands and New Caledonia in the Pacific Ocean. It includes three species. They are evergreen trees, related to *Dacrydium* and *Podocarpus*. Around the turn of the century *A. pancheri* was introduced into England. The species of *Acmopyle* look a little like *Taxus*. They are not of any importance to horticulture.

A. alba   A. pancheri   A. sahniana

Actinostrobus/CUPRESSACEAE

Actinostrobus is found only in the western part of Australia. The genus is related to the genus *Callitris*, also Australian, deviating from *Callitris* in the differently formed cones. There are three species known that are sometimes used as greenhouse plants. They are all erect growing trees; under less favorable conditions they become only pyramidal growing shrubs.

Actinostrobus is monoecious: the male "flowers" stand in catkins, or spikes; the female flowers are solitary and spherical with six scales. The seeds have three wings. The leaves are scale-like and grow in three rows; however, in the juvenile form needlelike is as common in many species of *Cupressaceae*. *Actinostrobus* is very rare and only of botanical interest.

A. acuminatus   A. arenarius   A. pyramidalis

Agathis/ARAUCARIACEAE

Agathis is a genus containing tall trees, found in the southeastern part of Asia: particularly the Philippines; large regions of Indonesia; the eastern part of Australia; the North Island of New Zealand; and Equatorial groups of islands in the Pacific Ocean.

The genus contains approximately 15 species, some of which can be seen in botanical gardens, where they are grown as tub plants. All *Agathis* species are evergreen. The leaves are lanceolate to ovate elliptical, fairly large, leathery, with parallel thin veins. They remain on the tree for several years.

Actinostrobus pyramidalis. Growing wild in Australia. This tropical species is never found in nurseries and is very rare in botanical gardens.

Some species are monoecious. The inflorescences are not important for this book, since *Agathis* in "captivity" rarely or never blooms.

A. australis is from New Zealand and was introduced into Europe in 1823; the best known species.

A. dammara is a useful tree because manila-copal, a form of resin that among others is used in the manufacturing of paint and varnish, is derived from it.

Most of the other species are not in cultivation and grow only in natural stands in the mountains of their natural habitat.

A. australis	*A. lanceolata*	*A. ovata*
A. borneensis	*A. microphylla*	*A. palmerstonii*
A. dammara	*A. microstachys*	*A. rhomboidalis*
A. flavescens	*A. moorei*	*A. robusta*
A. labillardieri	*A. obtusa*	*A. vitiensis*

Amentotaxus/TAXACEAE

Of *Amentotaxus* four species are known, all native to southern China. As far as is known, none of these species is in cultivation in Europe or America, only present in a few herbaria (Kew). They are evergreen shrubs or small trees, looking a little like *Cephalotaxus*. They differ from the latter in their different inflorescence and fruits. All species are dioecious; the seeds have a hard husk and a reddish seed coat, so that they look like a drupe.

A. argotaenia	*A. formosana*
A. cathayensis	*A. yunnanensis*

Araucaria/ARAUCARIACEAE

The genus *Araucaria* contains approximately 20 species, mostly from the tropical regions around the equator; New Guinea, Australia, New Zealand, New Caledonia and the Fiji Islands. Some species are native to South America, including the well-known *A. auracana*, that is at home in the Andes of west Brazil, Chile and Argentina. They are tall evergreen trees. Their branches are arranged in whorls on the trunk. Young shoots have no clearly visible buds. The leaves have an unusual shape and are scattered in two rows. *Araucaria* is mostly dioecious.

The trees bear seed only when fully mature, so it is impossible to determine the sex until the tree has reached a considerable age and blossomed. The cones of most species are very large. These develop only in the upper part of the tree. The three best known species belong to the section *Colymbea* (1). These are *A. angustifolia*, *A. araucana* and *A. bidwillii*. One species, *A. klinkii*, is classified in the section *Intermedia* (2). The remaining species belong to the section *Eutacta* (3).

A. angustifolia has been in cultivation for a long time and can be found in western Europe as a greenhouse plant in botanical gardens. In Europe and North America it is also known as a "House Fir" or Norfolk Pine and is commonly cultivated as a houseplant. Several cultivars do exist, but are extremely rare, save for 'Elegans'.

By far the best known species is *A. araucana*, which under favorable conditions in mild climates can

Araucaria bidwillii (right) and *Pinus pinea* (left). Commonly cultivated in tropical areas. The native name of *A. bidwillii* is Bunya-Bunya. (91)

develop into a nice tree. An often used but invalid name is *A. imbricata*. This species is sometimes called Monkey Puzzle.

A. bidwillii can be seen fairly often in older parks and gardens in the Mediterranean and other subtropical regions.

The remaining species are present sporadically in botanical collections but are not in commercial cultivation.

A. araucana is used for timber in South America, but on a very limited scale. The tree is classified as an 'endangered species' and it is no longer allowed to trade them from wild collected seed or as dug plants. Any shipment of *Araucaria araucana* must be accompanied by a certificate declaring that they have been raised in a nursery, from seed, harvested in gardens or nurseries.

A. angustifolia
A. araucana
A. balansae
A. beccarii
A. bernieri
A. bidwillii
A. biramulata
A. columnaris
A. cunninghamii
A. heterophylla
A. humboldtensis
A. klinkii
A. luxurians
A. montana
A. muelleri
A. rulei

Athrotaxus/TAXODIACEAE

Three species of this genus are known in Tasmania. They are all in cultivation in western Europe, but only in the mildest regions are they more or less hardy. All of them are trees; *A. selaginoides* can grow to 35 m in its native habitat. At first glance they look like *Thujopsis* and even a little like *Cryptomeria*, but they are not related to either. All species are monoecious. The cones look like those of *Cryptomeria* and ripen in one year. *A. cupressoides* has close contiguous scales, approximately 3 mm long. The other species have more needlelike leaves. The shape of the leaves of *A. laxifolia* is an intermediate between the leaves of *A. cupressoides* and *A. selaginoides*.

A. cupressoides
A. laxifolia
A. selanginoides

Austrocedrus/CUPRESSACEAE

Austrocedrus chilensis is split off from the larger and very heterogenous genus *Libocedrus*. This small tree is native to the southern part of the Andes. Even so *A. chilensis* is not hardy in cooler climates. Therefore, it must be overwintered in a cold greenhouse. The plants are monoecious; the cones are small and consist of four scales. The leaves are scale-like and arranged in two rows, as in *Thuja*. It has little ornamental value, but is an interesting species for collectors.

A. chilensis

Athrotaxis cupressoides. Large tree in a garden in Ireland. Hardy only in warm climates. (35)

6

Austrotaxus/TAXACEAE

This is another monotypic genus (consisting of one species) that outwardly looks like *Podocarpus*. The seeds look more like those of *Taxus*. The leaves are needlelike, quite long, 8–10 cm. *A. spicata* is indigenous only in the mountains of New Caledonia, where it grows in the rainforest. As far as is known, *Austrotaxus* is not in cultivation in Europe or in America.

    A. spicata

Callitris/CUPRESSACEAE

Of the 14 known species in the genus *Callitris*, all are found in Australia, New Zealand and New Caledonia. They are not hardy in Europe or North America except in the mild ocean climates of southern France, Spain, the Black Sea, California and Florida. Botanical gardens in more northerly latitudes maintain them outside in the summer and in greenhouses in the winter. All *Callitris* species are at home in dry regions. All *Callitris* species are evergreen, the majority become trees, but some species grow shrub-like. The are monoecious. The cones are fairly small and usually round. The cones remain on the tree for 2–3 years.

Two sections in this genus are distinguished. All species save one, are classified in the section *Hexaclinis* (1). Only *C. macleyana* belongs to the section *Octoclinis* (2). There are no named cultivars. In their native habitat they are considered very valuable trees for timber. *C. columellaris* is widely distributed in eastern Australia, and used for timber production, as is *C. rhomboidea*. The wood is not attacked by termites. In Australia they are referred to as "Pine", not to be confused with *Pinus*, also "Pine".

C. baileyi	C. muelleri
C. canescens	C. neo-caledonica
C. columellaris	C. oblonga
C. drummondii	C. preissii
C. endlicheri	C. rhomboidea
C. macleyana	C. roei
C. monticola	C. sulcata

Calocedrus/CUPRESSACEAE

Three species now classified as *Calocedrus* formerly were included in *Libocedrus*. The three are in cultivation and *C. decurrens* is particularly common in parks and gardens. The species are native to the western part of North America, Taiwan and China (Yunnan Province and Hainan). They are large, evergreen trees with flat branches. The leaves are arranged as crosswise scales in four rows. *Calodedrus* is monoecious. The cones are approximately 2 cm long and ripen in the first year.

C. decurrens is hardy but can be seriously damaged in very cold winters by strong winds. The two other species are not hardy and must be overwintered in a frost free environment. Outwardly, *Calocedrus* looks like *Cupressus* and *Chamaecyparis* but the shape of the cone deviates so much that the difference is clear. *C. decurrens* grows on fertile soil together with *Abies concolor*, in the mountainous regions of Oregon, northern California and Nevada. The tree is widely cultivated but grows considerably larger in its habitat than in Europe. *C. decurrens* is especially conspicuous because of its columnar habit. Beautiful examples can be seen in the Westonbirt Arboretum in England and in Lausanne on the banks of Lake Geneva, Switzerland. Good-sized specimens are also present in Blijdenstein, Hilversum, Holland.

Some cultivars are in cultivation, of which 'Aureovariegata' is the best known. In this cultivar, yellow foliaged twigs appear over the entire plant. This striking tree has been in cultivation for almost 100 years. 'Green Pillar', a new introduction, is excellent and makes a stong pyramidal plant. *Calocedrus decurrens* has a different, less conical habit in southerly climates than in more northerly latitudes.

In North America *C. decurrens* is used for timber production.

    C. decurrens
    C. formosana
    C. macrolepis

Calocedrus decurrens. This tree, displaying the conical habit, was photographed in the San Bernardino mountains of southern California.

Cathaya/PINACEAE

A monotypic genus, closely related to *Pseudotsuga*, *Cathaya* is found only in China (Sichuan and Guangxi Provinces). The tree was discovered in May, 1955, by members of the Guangfu-Lingchwen expedition and described by Chun and Kuang. It is a tall, evergreen tree, with horizontally arranged branches. The needles look much like those of *Pseudotsuga*. The cones differ markedly from *Pseudotsuga*, but not so much that the "new" genus *Cathaya* may not be classified under *Pseudotsuga*. A very detailed description is included in the *Manual of Cultivated Conifers*.

Cathaya argyrophylla is not yet in cultivation in Europe or North America.

C. argyrophylla

Cedrus libani. The Cedars of Lebanon are now rare. Taurus Mountains, Turkey, at 1600 m elevation.

Cedrus/PINACEAE

The genus *Cedrus* consists of 4 species from the Mediterranean and the Himalayas. The Mediterranean species have been in cultivation since time immemorial. They have always been of great importance. They are evergreen, large trees often with an irregularly shaped crown. The bark is grayish black. The leaves are always needle-shaped standing together in tight clusters (fascicles). They remain on the tree for 3–5 years. The buds are small. The arrangement of the *Cedrus* needles is very much like that of *Larix*, but all *Larix* species are deciduous and the cones of *Larix* are also quite different.

The cedars are monoecious. The male inflorescences are erect, approx. 5 cm long. The female cones are reddish and smaller. A cedar in bloom is a beautiful sight. The cones are made up of round scales which grow into tightly closed cones, that ripen in the second or third year.

From all 4 species of *Cedrus* a number of cultivars have been selected, some very well known and commonly cultivated, others very rare. *Cedrus atlantica*, the Atlas Cedar, is probably the best known cedar in cultivation. The branches are oblique, erect; the crown of old trees is broadly pyramidal. The needles are gray greenish blue, less often dark green. In its natural habitat the crown of *C. atlantica* is often as flat as *C. libani*. The best known cultivar is *C. atlantica* 'Glauca' with steel-blue needles and the same habit. The cultivar has a number of distinct clones, several of which are available. Seedlings of the fine blue-needled types can be selected regularly, but should only be propagated vegetatively.

The blue-needled cedars are often better branched than the green Atlas Cedars. The yellow-needled cultivar 'Aurea', that stays much smaller, is fairly common in cultivation. Magnificent specimens of the weeping forms 'Pendula' and 'Glauca Pendula' can be seen in large gardens and parks. *Cedrus libani* is native to Lebanon and the Taurus Mountains. The crown of *C. libani* is round flatish, the needles are usually somewhat shorter and the cone position differs from *C. atlantica*. Many cultivars of *C. libani* are grown; one of the most beautiful is 'Sargentii', a creeping plant with grayish green needles. The natural variety *C. libani* var. *stenocoma* is intermediate in habit between *C. libani* and *C. atlantica*, has green needles and is quite hardy. *C. libani* can suffer in severe winters and is, therefore, not useful in the continental climate of central Europe and North America.

C. brevifolia grows only in, and is restricted to, the National Park on Cyprus. The tree is much smaller than *C. libani* and the needles much shorter.

C. deodara comes from the Himalayas. This species is not entirely hardy in the colder regions of Europe and North America. Many cultivars have been derived from this species. Some very nice forms are 'Aurea' with golden yellow needles; 'Pendula' with pendulous branches and 'Albospica' with white-yellow needles at the end of young twigs. Recently, some better and hardier cultivars have been developed in West Germany, such as 'Karl Fuchs' and 'Paktia'. The practical landscape use of these new cultivars remains to be seen.

Long before our era, the Cedars of Lebanon were of great importance for the building of palaces, temples and ships. The Phoenicians sailed the Mediterranean in ships made of cedar. In those days large areas of what is now Syria and Lebanon were covered with cedar forests. Cedars were also numerous in Turkey. Today they are very rare in their habitat and are firmly protected. Extinction need not be feared if the remaining forests are well protected. The World Nature Fund is participating in this conservation effort. Of all plants in the Bible, the Cedar of Lebanon is mentioned most often.

The native stands of *C. atlantica* in the Atlas Mountains have been significantly reduced in the last several hundred years. As in Lebanon, destruction of the forests for cultivation has taken its toll.

The cedars are totally unsuited for forestry in western Europe.

C. atlantica
C. brevifolia
C. deodara
C. libani

Cephalotaxus/CEPHALOTAXACEAE

Of the genus *Cephalotaxus* 8 species are known, 2 of which are in cultivation. Occasionally, one or two other species can be seen in botanical gardens. The native habitat of the *Cephalotaxus* species is confined to Asia, from the Himalayas to Japan. The species are evergreen; some become trees, others remain shrubby. Needles are shaped like those of *Taxus*, arranged in two rows and usually fairly aromatic to bitter smelling. All *Cephalotaxus* species are dioecious. The seeds are fairly large and drupe-like with a fleshy green coating which is brownish red on ripening. The seeds usually germinate the second year. *Cephalotaxus* looks in many ways like *Torreya*, but *Torreya* fruit looks more like a nut, but with a fleshy coat. Moreover, *Torreya* needles are sharp, while those of *Cephalotaxus* are blunt.

C. fortunei is shrub-like, has longer needles than *C. harringtonia* and is much rarer in cultivation. Unfor-

tunately, the long needled forms of *C. harringtonia* are labeled as *C. fortunei*. The needles of the true *C. fortunei* taper gradually to a sharp point, while those of *C. harringtonia* taper more directly to a blunt tip. *C. harringtonia* is native to Japan, Korea and northern China and is much hardier than *C. fortunei*.

Several cultivars have been developed. Very well known is *C. harringtonia* 'Fastigiata'; sometimes offered as *Podocarpus koraiana*. The form 'Prostrata' is valuable for its creeping habit. Large examples of this form can be seen at the entrance of the Gimborn-arboretum in Doorn, The Netherlands.

C. fortunei
C. griffithii
C. hainanensis
C. harringtonia
C. mannii
C. oliveri
C. sinensis
C. wilsoniana

Chamaecyparis/CUPRESSACEAE

Chamaecyparis is perhaps the most important conifer genus in horticulture. Hundreds of cultivars have been developed from only a few species. Seven species are known, which inhabit North America, Japan, Taiwan and China.

The North American *C. lawsoniana* is the parent of an enormous number of cultivars, varying from small dwarf forms to large trees and with many color nuances. This species, the natural distribution of which covers a surprisingly small area, is found only in the mountains of southern Oregon and in northwestern California in the United States. The species apparently mutates very easily in cultivation as do a few other species, including *Thuja occidentalis*, *Picea abies* and some *Juniperus* species. In its natural habitat *Chamaecyparis lawsoniana* demonstrates none of this variability.

C. nootkatensis, also from the coastal region of the Pacific Northwest is much less variable; the number of cultivars is limited to about 15. The best known is *C. nootkatensis* 'Pendula', a beautiful garden form. This weeping tree is a fixed adult form of the species. In nature one sees that the top part of the mature trees takes on this weeping form. There are at least two different forms in the trade with this same name; a densely growing form, and another, more graceful and open.

The Japanese *C. obtusa* is also the origin of many cultivars, varying from small dwarf forms to large trees. Japanese gardeners have selected from this species for hundreds of years, as they have from *C.*

pisifera from which tens of cultivars have been selected. Less well known is *C. thyoides,* from the southeastern part of North America. A well-known cultivar is *C. thyoides* 'Andelyensis', a grayish green cone-shaped dwarf form.

Neither *C. funebris* (formerly *Cupressus funebris*) nor *C. formosensis* are hardy in temperate climates but can be grown in the Mediterranean climates.

All species of *Chamaecyparis* are monoecious. The male cones are small and usually yellow. The female cones are small and spherical, usually ripening in the first year. The leaves in the juvenile stage are blunt needlelike, becoming scaly later.

Spach split the genus *Chamaecyparis* from *Cupressus,* first established by Linnaeus. The species of *Chamaecyparis* differ from *Cupressus* mainly in the form of the cones. In *Cupressus* they are larger, and ripen only in the second or third year. The arrangement of the leaves also differs between the two genera. In earlier years there was much confusion over the derivation of various cultivars, which bore only needlelike leaves, not the typical scale-like leaves of mature plants. It is now recognized that many cultivars belonging to *C. pisifera* were classified under the "genus" *Retinospora.* This old synonym has now fallen out of use completely.

Chamaecyparis is not an important forestry tree in Europe, but in the United States *C. lawsoniana* and *C. nootkatensis* are widely planted for timber production.

C. formosensis	C. obtusa
C. funebris	C. pisifera
C. lawsoniana	C. thyoides
C. nootkatensis	

Cryptomeria/TAXODIACEAE

A monotypic genus, native to Japan and China, *Cryptomeria japonica* has provided a large number of cultivars, most coming from Japan. *Cryptomeria* is a very important forestry tree in Japan, as well as being of great importance in Japanese horticulture. Because *C. japonica* is quite variable, constantly forming new sports or mutations, a large number of cultivars have been developed. Many of these cultivars have found places in the gardens of North America and Europe.

C. japonica grows to 30–40 m tall in Japan, but is lower in cultivation. It forms a bolt upright trunk with an open, narrow crown. The leaves are sickle-shaped, placed in 5 rows, spirally arranged. The bark comes off in strips and is reddish brown. *C. japonica* is monoecious; the cones are small with a diameter of approx. 1–1.5 cm and spherical. After the seeds have

Chamaecyparis lawsoniana. Very well-known species of which a large number of cultivars are in cultivation. (21)

dropped, the cones stay on the trees. Kruse mentions a tree in Japan that was 64 m tall in 1968 and had a trunk diameter of 7 m.

Japanese horticulture recognizes a large number of cultivars which have been given partially Japanese and partially Latin cultivar names. Many of them are no longer in cultivation. Several forms are in cultivation in Japan that were formerly unknown in Europe. Some have recently been introduced, among others 'Rasen-sugi'. Contrariwise there are some cultivars of European origin unknown in Japan, e.g. 'Vilmoriniana'.

Some excellent cultivars are 'Cristata,' a small tree of which the branches and twigs form many fascicles or cockscombs; 'Compacta,' a tall growing slender tree with compact cone-shaped crown; 'Jindai-sugi,' a short-needled compact pyramidal growing form; 'Globosa Nana,' a flat round shape; 'Elegans,' turns copper-red in the winter. Most cultivars are hardy in the colder regions of Europe and North America. Almost all cultivars can be grown in mild temperate climates.

Cryptomeria is of no importance in forestry outside Japan.

C. japonica

Cunninghamia/TAXODIACEAE

In the genus *Cunninghamia* 3 species are known, of which 2 are from Taiwan and 1 from China. In their native habitat *Cunninghamia* become large, evergreen trees with a narrow cone-shaped crown. The leaves are lanceolate, stiff and fairly sharply pointed. *Cunninghamia* is monoecious; the cones are 3–4 cm long, the cone-scales are separated from each other and are arranged imbricately. In mild temperature regions *Cunninghamia* grows well, becoming large trees. In the colder locations they usually remain as small, irregularly shaped, and shrub-like trees. In continental climates they usually suffer badly.

By far the best known species is *C. lanceolata* with light green needles. From this species the greyish green-blue cultivar 'Glauca' has been developed that is hardier than the species. This form is sometimes mistaken for *C. konishii*, which is much more sensitive to frost. Good specimens of *C. lanceolata* can be seen in many arboreta and botanic gardens.

C. kawakamii   *C. konishii*   *C. lanceolata*

Cupressocyparis leylandii 'Naylor's Blue'. The 'bluest' of all, but difficult to propagate. (1)

Cupressocyparis/CUPRESSACEAE

Cupressocyparis is an infraspecific genus of hybrids between *Cupressus* and *Chamaecyparis*, that accidently sprang up in cultivation. Dallimore described this group and introduced the name. They all become large trees, with a compact, pyramidal habit. They are very well suited for the making of high, dense hedges and wind breakers.

The best known hybrid is *C.* × *leylandii* a cross between *Chamaecyparis nootkatensis* and *Cupressus macrocarpa*.

Around 1910, J. M. Naylor (Leighton Hall, Welshpool, U.K.) introduced the first clone of which *Cupressus macrocarpa* was the mother tree. Many years before, C. J. Leyland had grown a similar hybrid, of which *Chamaecyparis nootkatensis* was the mother tree. This selection was never introduced. Years later this hybrid was bred again in Stapehill, Dorset, U.K. Several clones were selected from these seedlings that are now propagated in large quantities. Especially well known are 'Haggerston Grey' and 'Leighton Green'. The golden yellow 'Castlewellan Gold' sprang up accidentally in 1963 from seed of *C.* × *leylandii*. The difficult to propagate bluish 'Naylor's Blue' recalls the founder of this important group.

C. leylandii   *C. notabilis*   *C. ovensii*

Cupressus/CUPRESSACEAE

The genus *Cupressus* contains approx. 20 species, some of which have been in cultivation for centuries. Some species are native to the Mediterranean. Thus, *C. sempervirens* frequently determines the appearance of many gardens and landscapes in that region.

Some species are native to the Himalayas and North America. All are evergreen, medium tall trees, only rarely shrubs, except in unfavorable conditions. The leaves are scale-like, small and standing closely together. The cypresses are monoecious. The cones are hard and round, and ripen in the second year.

The most hardy of the species is *C. arizonica (C. glabra)*. The most common, most hardy cultivar is *C. arizonica* 'Conica' (also often labeled as "Glauca"), a fairly broad columnar form with steel-blue, scale-like leaves.

C. cashmeriana is perhaps the most beautiful species, but not at all hardy except in the mildest locations.

C. lusitanica is not native to Portugal as the name suggests, but rather to Mexico.

The Monterey Cypress (*C. macrocarpa*) or 'Lambert', as it is called in France, is a widely planted species for windbreaks in regions with a fairly mild

Cupressus macrocarpa. Called Lambert Cypress in France. Native to southern California, but widely planted in Europe. Here a tree on the Monterey Peninsula, U.S.A.

climate, such as Brittany, southern England, California, etc.

The cultivar 'Goldcrest' is a soft yellow form, cultivated by the hundreds of thousands as a coniferous houseplant. The Italian Cypress, *C. sempervirens* has been cultivated and planted since time immemorial, and is only hardy in southern Europe and the milder regions of North America. The well-known columnar form 'Stricta' is cultivated on a large scale in France and Italy.

C. abramsiana	C. guadalupensis
C. arizonica	C. lusitanica
C. bakeri	C. macnabiana
C. cashmeriana	C. macrocarpa
C. duclouxiana	C. sargentii
C. forbesii	C. sempervirens
C. goveniana	C. torulosa

Dacrydium/PODOCARPACEAE

This genus includes 17 species, all native to New Zealand, Tasmania, New Caledonia, Taiwan, Borneo and, strangely enough, one species in Chile. They are evergreen trees or shrubs, closely related to *Podocarpus*. All species are dioecious, the seeds are egg-shaped with a fleshy cover. The leaves are usually small, often scale-like.

None of the species are hardy in any save subtropical climates. Most species are in cultivation in botanical gardens.

Two species form low, creeping little shrubs. *D. cupressinum* barely reaches a half meter tall. *D. laxifolium* grows at the most 10 cm high, but can grow meter-long branches along the ground.

D. araucarioides	D. biforme
D. balansae	D. colensoi
D. bidwillii	D. cupressinum

D. elatum	D. kirkii
D. fonkii	D. laxifolium
D. franklinii	D. lycopodioides
D. intermedium	

Diselma/CUPRESSACEAE

A monotypic genus, closely related to *Fitzroya*; *Diselma archeri* is present only in the mountains on the west side of Tasmania. It is a shrub to 150 cm tall, rarely taller. The leaves are scale-like and tightly packed. The species is dioecious. The cones are very small.

D. archeri can be obtained in a few nurseries in Europe and North America. The ornamental value of the plant is slight, and its hardiness leaves much to be desired.

   D. archeri

Fitzroya/CUPRESSACEAE

Fitzroya is a monotypic genus. In its native habitat of southern Chile and Patagonia, these plants become tall trees, to 35 m high, and very large in diameter. *Fitzroya* is monoecious, the cones are small, 6–8 mm long. The leaves are needlelike, and are arranged in three rows, somewhat outspread and 3–4 mm long. The bark is conspicuously brownish red.

Some individuals become very old; trees up to 2000 years old have been reported. In the mild regions of England, Ireland and temperate North America, *Fitzroya* is reasonably hardy, elsewhere it is only a greenhouse plant. *Fitzroya* is a protected species.

   F. cupressoides

Fokienia/CUPRESSACEAE

Of the genus *Fokienia* 3 species are known, all native to China. According to the latest taxonomic opinions, the 3 species all are *F. hodginsii*. Thus, it is a monotypic genus. At first glance, *Fokienia* looks like *Thujopsis dolabrata*. However, the cones clearly differ from either because of their pear shape. *Fokienia* is very rare, even in botanical collections. The tree is only hardy in the mildest regions of England, Ireland, Brittany and California.

F. hodginsii

Glyptostrobus/TAXODIACEAE

Another monotypic genus, native to southeastern China, the plant closely resembles *Taxodium* or *Metasequoia*. It becomes a moderately large tree, deciduous, but differing from *Taxodium* in differently shaped cones. *Glyptostrobus* is monoecious, the cone-scales lie imbricate over each other. The leaves are needlelike, pectinately arranged as in *Metasequoia* or *Taxodium*. It is not hardy but in the mildest regions. *Glyptostrobus* survives only in the mildest regions of Europe and North America. The tree is possibly extinct in the wild, but is cultivated widely in China, especially along rice paddies. There they form aerial roots.

G. lineatus

Juniperus/CUPRESSACEAE

The large genus *Juniperus* contains approximately 60 species, and hundreds of cultivars are recognized. No cultivars are known of many of the species, and several species are seldom or never cultivated. The habitat of *Juniperus* includes all of the Northern Hemisphere, from the polar regions to the tropical mountains. *Juniperus* can also be found in Greenland, Iceland, and even in Northern Siberia. *Juniperus communis* is the species with the most extensive area of distribution, appearing in many varieties from the north to the mountains of northern Africa.

All species of *Juniperus* are evergreen. They form good sized shrubs to fairly large trees. The former are frequently recumbent or creeping and can cover large areas. The branching is irregular and spreading. The leaves are needlelike or scale-like; both leaf types often appear on the same plant (*J. chinensis*). On the contrary the leaves of *J. communis* are always needle-like, or better put awl-like. Some species are monoecious, others dioecious. The cones are always very small. Clouds of pollen literally fly from the male flowers. The seeds are grouped together in so-called coneberries. Fleshy connated scales cover the hard seeds that usually ripen in the first year and are usually dark blue. The berries of *J. communis* are a valuable condiment used for many purposes.

The coneberry distinguishes *Juniperus* from other genera of the *Cupressaceae*, which all bear dry cones.

Linnaeus described *J. communis* in the first edition of his work *Species Plantarum*. Gaussen published a taxonomical classification of the genus in 3 subgenera which is reproduced here in brief. The subgenus *Caryocedrus* (1) contains only the tree-like *J. drupaceae*. The subgenus *Oxycedrus* (2) is divided into three sections: that is, Section *Oxycedroides* (a) containing 5 Asian species, e.g. *J. cedrus* and *J. oxycedrus*, found around the Mediterranean Sea; the Section *Rigidoides* (b) including the common *J. communis*, the Asian *J. procumbens* and *J. rigida*; finally the Section *Recurvoides* (c) with four Asian species, e.g. *J. squamata*. The third subgenus is *Sabina* (3), divided in 6 sections, containing all remaining species.

In the Section *Phoenicioides* (a) belong all the central Asian species; in the Section *Pachyphlaeoides* (b) several American and Mexican species, just as in the Section *Occidentalis* (c). In the Section *Excelsoides* (d) some rather uncommon species from Africa and the Middle East are combined. The Section *Chinensioides* (e) contains, e.g., *J. chinensis* and *J. sabina*. Last is the Section *Virginioides* (f) with American species like *J. horizontalis*, *J. scopulorum* and *J. virginiana*.

Several species are very rare in cultivation. Many species are hardy in the colder regions of Europe and North America. In every arboretum of any size a collection of species and cultivars of *Juniperus* is planted.

The many cultivars derive from only about 10 species. The cultivars often much better satisfy landscaping requirements in parks and private gardens than the species. Many cultivars of the most widely distributed species *J. communis* are grown. It should be noted that some cultivars are selections collected in nature and then propagated vegetatively (e.g. *J. communis* var. *depressa* and the cultivars 'Depressed Star' and 'Vase'). *J. communis* varies markedly in appearance from shrub- or columnar-like to creeping, depending on the habitat of the variety. A very well-known and valued columnar form is *J. communis* 'Suecica'; widely cultivated creeping cultivars are 'Repanda' and 'Horni-brookii'.

Several common cultivars derived from *J. chinensis* are used in landscaping. Many cultivars formerly assigned to *J. chinensis* are now included in *J.* × *media*, a hybrid group of *J. chinensis* and *J. sabina*. The name, *J.*

× *media,* was given by Van Melle in 1947 although Dmitrov had used this name earlier for a hybrid, namely *J. semiglobosa* × *J. turkestanica.* It has recently been proposed to use for this group the name *Juniperus* × *Pfitzeriana,* so that names such as *J. pfitzeriana* 'Plumosa Aurea' or *J. pfitzeriana* 'Hetsii' etc., can be used. The widely used name *J.* × *media* is used in this survey, although it may be rejected in the future. Moreover, several cultivars, now classified as *J.* × *media* do not show any influence of *J. sabina.* This matter is quite complex and cannot be solved in a book like this.

J. sabina has been in cultivation since antiquity. It has for centuries been important in medical science. It is a very poisonous tree. Many cultivars exist, of which 'Tamariscifolia' is the most widespread. Cultivars like the more erect growing 'Hicksii' and the new 'Broadmoor' are derived from this species.

J. scopulorum is satisfactory only in continental climates. In regions of high humidity and in damp climates the plant loses many leaves.

J. squamata, a Chinese species, is the parent of some well-known newer forms such as 'Blue Star' and 'Blue Carpet' and of course also of the older 'Meyeri'.

Cultivars of *J. horizontalis* are horticulturally very important, particularly 'Wiltonii', grayish blue, carpet-like, and the new 'Emerald Spreader', more grayish green.

J. virginiana, originating in North America, is called Red Cedar and is a very valuable timber tree. Many cultivars have been developed, some shrub-like, mostly tree-like, including 'Canaertii', a nice dark green and 'Glauca', with steel-blue scales.

Cultivars from some less well-known species, such as *J. davurica* and *J. procumbens* are also in cultivation.

Some species are important for timber production—e.g. *J. virginiana.* The wood of some Asian species is used for the production of small objects.

J. ashei	*J. occidentalis*
J. barbadensis	*J. osteosperma*
J. bermudiana	*J. oxycedrus*
J. brevifolia	*J. phoenicia*
J. californica	*J. pinchotii*
J. cedrus	*J. potaninii*
J. centrasiatica	*J. procera*
J. chinensis	*J. procumbens*
J. communis	*J. przewalskii*
J. conferta	*J. pseudosabina*
J. convallium	*J. ramulosa*
J. davurica	*J. recurva*
J. deppeana	*J. rigida*
J. distans	*J. sabina*
J. drupacea	*J. saltuaria*
J. durangensis	*J. sargentii*
J. excelsa	*J. scopulorum*
J. flaccida	*J. semiglobosa*
J. foetidissima	*J. seravshanica*
J. formosana	*J. silicicola*
J. glaucescens	*J. squamata*
J. horizontalis	*J. taxifolia*
J. kansuensis	*J. thurifera*
J. komarovii	*J. tibetica*
J. macrocarpoda	*J. turkestanica*
J. × *media*	*J. virginiana*
J. mekongensis	*J. wallichiana*
J. monosperma	*J. zaidamensis*
J. morrisonicola	

Juniperus communis. Old plants on the Luenenburger Heide, Germany. The common Juniper Berry is native to Western Europe.

Keteleeria/PINACEAE

4–8 species are numbered in the genus *Keteleeria*, depending on the vision of the various taxonomists. They are tall, evergreen trees growing in dry regions in China and on Taiwan. The leaves of *Keteleeria* look like those of *Abies*, as do the cones, but unlike *Abies*, abscise completely.

Keteleeria is very rarely seen in cultivation in the west. *K. evelyniana* forms beautiful trees, which are planted for horticultural purposes in China—notably around the city of Kunming in Yunnan Province.

K. chien peii
K. cyclolepsis
K. davidiana
K. esquirolii
K. evelyniana
K. fortunei
K. roullettii

Larix/PINACEAE

The genus *Larix* includes 10 species, all deciduous and found widely distributed around the Northern Hemisphere. *Larix* species form vast and economically important forests, particularly in Canada and Siberia. The leaves are soft and thin. All *Larix* species are monoecious; the juvenile cones are conspicuously purple-red. Ripe cones are fairly small and stay on the tree after the seeds have dropped.

The species of *Larix* are difficult to distinguish by vegetative characteristics. The taxonomy of *Larix* includes almost as many sections as species.

In Central Europe *Larix decidua* forms large forests in Austria and Italy on high plateaus. Large *Larix* forests are also located in the Engadin region of Switzerland. In Poland, and also the Carpathian mountains, a different variety, *L. decidua* var. *polonica*, is found. The Japanese *L. kaempferi*, better known as *L. leptolepis*, is frequently planted in western European forests. However, the hybrid *L.* × *eurolepis* is better suited for forestry. The seeds of these species are harvested from special "seed orchards" maintained for the production of seed for reforestation. The F_1 hybrid *L.* × *eurolepis* is a very vigorous forest tree.

Two important species are found in America, *L. laricina* and *L. occidentalis*. Neither species is of great importance elsewhere so they are only present in some collections. *L. russica*, growing in Siberia, even though completely hardy, is not of any particular importance as a garden plant.

Cultivars have been derived from some *Larix* spp. Of these, the so-called Weeping Larix, *L. kaempferi* 'Pendula' is the best known.

Branches with cones are sold in large quantities for Christmas decorations.

L. decidua	L. lyallii
L. gmelinii	L. mastersiana
L. griffithiana	L. occidentalis
L. kaempferi	L. potaninii
L. laricina	L. russica

Larix decidua. The autumn colors of the *Larix* forests in the central European mountains are magnificent. Near Zirl, Austria.

Libocedrus/CUPRESSACEAE

The genus *Libocedrus* was formerly made up of 13 species so different from one another that revision of the genus in 1926, 1930, 1953 and 1954 divided them into 5 new genera. If these revisions are accepted, only 5 species remain in *Libocedrus*; the 8 other species are classified under *Calocedrus*, *Austrocedrus*, *Papuacedrus* and *Pilgerodendron*.

Scientifically this splitting is justified, even though it is not generally accepted. In practice this is not too

15

important, since most species are not in cultivation.

The 5 remaining species now included in the genus are evergreen trees with flat twigs and scale-like leaves. The seeds are winged and develop in small cones. All species are native to New Zealand and New Caledonia and none is at all hardy. In warm climates *L. bidwillii* can be seen but rarely.

L. austro-caledonica   L. plumosa
L. bidwillii   L. yateensis
L. chevalieri

Metasequoia/TAXODIACEAE

Metasequoia is a monotypic genus, living examples of which have not been known very long. The genus was first described from fossil findings. In 1941, Lung-skin Yang discovered in the remote Shui-Hsa-Pa Valley in southeast China remarkable deciduous trees unknown to him. First they were though to be *Glyptostrobus lineatus*, but soon branches and cones were collected and correlated with the material that previously had been known only through fossils. It was not until 1946, after the upheavals of World War II, that seed was received by the Arnold Arboretum. In 1947 the first seeds arrived in Europe.

Metasequoia is a large deciduous tree, appearing much like *Taxodium*. Another point of similarity with *Taxodium* is the fact that the young branchlets fall off with the needles. It differs from the latter in the differently formed cones and opposite leaf arrangement. Even without leaves *Metasequoia* are easy to identify by their elliptical to ovate, yellowish brown buds that stand away from the branches.

Stands outside of China are very uniform because *Metasequoia* is generally propagated from cuttings. It is true that the trees in the Occident originated from seeds, but this species is now grown from cuttings.

In the Netherlands almost all trees orignated from a clone grown in the Botanical Gardens of the University of Utrecht. This tree is still standing in the Sortimentsgarden of the Research Station for Arboriculture in Boskoop and is widely distributed all over Europe.

M. glyptostroboides

Microbiota/CUPRESSACEAE

Microbiota is a monotypic genus that only recently has become common in cultivation, although known in the literature for 50 years. It was first thought to be very closely related to *Juniperus*. It is a flat growing,

densely branched, evergreen shrub, not higher than about 50 cm but several meters wide. The leaves are scale-like, very small, and triangular, much like *Chamaecyparis*. In the winter the foliage is a purple-brown color, in the summer fresh green.

Although alleged to be dioecious, *Microbiota* is actually monoecious. Small female cones developed for the first time on vegetatively propagated plants in 1979 in the Arboretum Trompenburg in Rotterdam. These seeds were carefully collected and sown. They produced about 50 plants that first bore juvenile needles, but later formed scale-like leaves and differed in no way from the parent. The species was collected in the wild by Komarov. It was first cultivated in the Botanical Gardens of Tashkent, Uzbekistan, USSR. From there plants from cuttings were brought to Hannover-Muenden via Czechoslovakia. Cuttings from Hannover were sent to Rotterdam in 1968. At the 1976 "Flora Nova" Exhibition in Boskoop they were exhibited and received an honorary award. In 1976 they were put on the market in the Netherlands and distributed throughout Europe.

Microbiota is native to the eastern part of Siberia, in the vicinity of Vladivostok.

The plant is completely hardy.

M. decussata

Metasequoia glyptostroboides. A deciduous conifer discovered in 1942 and now widely distributed. Good street tree. (79)

Microcachrys/PODOCARPACEAE

Microcachrys is a monotypic genus from Tasmania, where it grows as a low evergreen shrub in the mountains in damp, peaty bogs. The branches are square (4-sided), the leaves are very small and scale-like. *Microcachrys* is dioecious, the seeds grow in a cone that looks like a mulberry. As far as is known, this species is not yet in cultivation.

    M. tetragona

Microstrobos/PODOCARPACEAE

The genus *Microstrobos* contains 2 species native to Australia and Tasmania. They are evergreen shrubs, related to *Diselma* and *Microcachrys,* and like them love moist sites with high humidity. The leaves are scale-like, the cones are small and develop on short shoots.

    Neither species is in cultivation in Europe as they are not at all hardy. They are cultivated in Australia, New Zealand and the subtropical regions of North America.

    M. fitzgeraldii
    M. niphophilus

Neocallitropsis/CUPRESSACEAE

A monotypic genus, found in New Caledonia. It is a medium tall tree to 10 m high. Leaves are scale-like, looking somewhat like *Callitris* and *Cryptomeria*. The species is not in cultivation and has been found only once, in 1914, in the mountains of New Caledonia.
N. araucarioides

Papuacedrus/CUPRESSACEAE

Papuacedrus is one of the genera split off from *Libocedrus*. These are tall trees with scale-like leaves, from New Guinea. Three species are known, but are not widely cultivated. Several plants are in cultivation in the Royal Botanic Gardens in Edinburgh and Kew.

    P. arfakensis
    P. papuana
    P. torricellensis

Phyllocladus/PHYLLOCLADACEAE

The genus *Phyllocladus* contains 5 species, all of which are native to the islands of Southeast Asia, New Zealand and Tasmania. They are evergreen trees or shrubs with long shoots and leaf-like short shoots. They are mono- or dioecious; the seed has a hard shell. None of the species is hardy and they are very rarely found in cultivation. A garden form of *P. alpinus,* native to New Zealand, 'Silver Blades' is in cultivation.

P. alpinus	*P. hypophyllus*
P. asplenifolius	*P. trichomanoides*
P. glaucus	

Picea/PINACEAE

Of the large genus *Picea* about 50 species are known, depending on the opinion of the botanist to whom one talks. About 250 cultivars have been derived from only a limited number of species. No cultivars have come from most of the species and in fact many of the species are not in cultivation at all.

    Picea is an extraordinarily widely distributed genus. Species are found over the entire Northern Hemisphere, usually in forests. Only a few *Picea* are native to southwestern Europe. None exists in Africa, the Middle East or southwestern Asia. Genuine tropical species are unknown. All *Picea* species are evergreen. They are usually tall trees with long, upright stems. In dense forests foliage is found only at the top. The branches are radiate. The bark of most species is rough and "scale-like", sometimes also furrowed. The leaves are needlelike and usually arranged in two rows, although sometimes radially placed around the twig, as in *P. pungens* and *P. engelmannii.* The underside of the needles is usually silver-blue or greenish blue. The buds are brown and without resin. All species are monoecious. The male cones are seated in the axils of the upper leaves; the female at the end of the previous year's twigs. The cones are pendulous, varying widely in size and do not drop off as a whole. Another practical means of identifying *Picea* species is that, when a needle is carefullly pulled off, a piece of the twig epidermis always tears off with it.

    Linnaeus included *Picea* with *Abies, Larix,* etc., etc., etc. in the genus *Pinus.* This classification was not sustainable, so Dietrich split *Picea* into a separate genus. A piquant taxonomic detail: Linnaeus called the well-known Christmas tree or Ornamental Spruce, *Pinus abies.* When Dietrich described *Picea,* and Miller *Abies,* a name like *Picea abies* was not allowed according to the then valid rules. So Link called European Ornamental Spruce *Picea excelsa,* still today a much used name. When the use of older genus names as a specific epithet was again allowed, the priority rules dictated that the valid species name

Picea omorika. Growing in the wild near Stolac, Yugoslavia. Every connoisseur of conifers recognizes this species immediately by its habit.

must conform to the oldest description. Karstens, therefore, published the name *Picea abies* (Linnaeus) Karst.

Picea is now subdivided into 3 sections. The section *Picea* (1) contains at least 20 species found throughout the entire distribution area. Some of the better known species in this section are *P. abies, P. asperata, P. glauca, P. orientalis, P. polita, P. rubens* and *P. smithiana.* The section *Casicta* (2) includes the species in which the needles are arranged radially around the twig. These species are native to North America and eastern Asia: *P. jezoensis, P. likiangensis, P. montigena, P. pungens,* etc. The section *Omorika* (3) includes only 4 species, two of which are very well-known, *P. breweriana* and *P. omorika,* the Serbian Spruce.

Some species are very well suited for use in not-too-large gardens, among others, *P. omorika, P. orientalis* and *P. pungens* with their various shapes. Most species are not well suited for general use and are, therefore, only rarely present in cultivation, except in collections.

Many cultivars have been developed from *Picea abies* that are very satisfactory as garden plants, as are the cultivars of *P. glauca, P. mariana, P. orientalis,* and *P. pungens.* Many of these cultivars are used on a large scale. Some natural varieties of *Picea abies* such as *P. abies* 'Pendula Major' and *P. abies* 'Viminalis' are vegetatively propagated. Several forms which originated in the wild as witches'-brooms and have been collected and preserved by nurserymen. Some good dwarf forms are 'Nidiformis', 'Ohlendorffii', 'Pumila Nigra' and 'Repens'. 'Cranstonii' is also a very striking tree with only a few branches and large coarse needles and buds. The well-known *P. glauca* 'Conica' is cultivated and sold by the hundreds of thousands. In the United States this dwarf form is used as "second" Christmas tree. *P. glauca* 'Echiniformis' is also an excellent garden plant; it is a very slow growing dwarf form, suited for the rock garden.

P. likiangensis var. *balfouriana,* from western China, is a beautiful silver-gray, pyramidal tree. *P. mariana* 'Beissneri' was widely cultivated at the beginning of this century but is now less well-known, but still valuable. *P. omorika* is cultivated on a large scale, especially in Germany. A dwarf form originating in the Netherlands is 'Nana', a witches'-broom found by Goudkade Bros. in Boskoop.

The Caucasian Spruce, *P. orientalis,* is an elegant tree, with very short needles and small cones. The cultivar 'Atrovirens' has dark green needles; 'Aurea' comes out golden yellow but turns green in the summer. 'Early Gold' also comes out yellow but remains a greenish yellow.

Perhaps the best known spruce is *P. pungens* var. *glauca,* the Blue Spruce, that appears in all sorts of forms and colors. *P. breweriana,* one of the most beautiful spruce species, is found exclusively in the Siskiyou Mountains in northern California, U.S.A. where they are fiercely protected. Only several hundred trees are left and regeneration is slow. Cultivated specimens of *P. breweriana* are much nicer than the congeners found in the wild.

Many *Picea* species are extremely important in forestry. In Europe, *P. abies* is planted on a large scale and also found in large natural stands. Not only is a great deal of lumber in the building industry derived from *P. abies,* but also firewood, paper pulp and Christmas trees. Millions are cultivated for the latter purpose. *P. abies* grows best in a cool site with high humidity and cool permeable sandy or clay soil. *P. abies* is often planted in an unsuitable location which accounts for wholesale forest mortality in some localities that is incorrectly attributed to acid rain.

On the west coast of America *P. engelmannii* is an important forest tree. In Canada, near the Pacific coast, *P. glauca* is an important species as is *P. sitchensis* in Alaska. The latter species does not thrive in

Pinus aristata var. *longaeva*. This *Pinus* is the oldest living organism on earth. The age is, with some accuracy, estimated at about 4600 years.

Europe except in some localities in Great Britain.

P. abies	*P. meyeri*
P. alcoquiana	*P. montigena*
P. asperata	*P. morrisonicola*
P. aurantiaca	*P. neoveitchii*
P. brachytyla	*P. obovata*
P. breweriana	*P. omorika*
P. chihuahuana	*P. orientalis*
P. engelmannii	*P. polita*
P. gemmata	*P. pungens*
P. glauca	*P. pungsaniensis*
P. glehnii	*P. retroflexa*
P. hirtella	*P. rubens*
P. jezoensis	*P. schrenkiana*
P. koyamai	*P. sitchensis*
P. likiangensis	*P. smithiana*
P. mariana	*P. spinulosa*
P. maximowiczii	*P. wilsonii*
P. mexicana	

Pilgerodendron/CUPRESSACEAE

This is another monotypic genus separated from *Libocedrus*. The species is an evergreen tree, sometimes tall, under poor conditions a shrub. It is native to the Andes mountains in Chile.

Pilgerodendron is dioecious; the cones have 4 scales, the leaves are very small and tightly appressed.

This tree can be cultivated in a cool greenhouse in cold climates.

P. uviferum

Pinus/PINACEAE

The genus *Pinus* contains 70–100 species, again depending on the opinion of various taxonomists. They grow in the Northern Hemisphere, above the polar circle in Europe and North America and southward to the mountains of Central America, North Africa, Indochina and north Sumatra.

Most species from tropical and subtropical regions are not hardy in cooler climates.

All *Pinus* species are evergreen. Most develop into trees, though some species grow shrub-like in the mountains of Europe, North America, China and Japan, e.g. *Pinus mugo* in Europe and *P. pumila* in Japan. The leaves are needlelike, arranged in fascicles of 2–8; the number of needles per fascicle is species-specific. All species are monoecious; the male "flowers" are axillary on the side shoots, while the female "flowers" are on the terminals. Cones vary in shape, often ovate or globose, usually asymmetrical.

The cones remain on the tree to ripen in the second or third year and then burst open. In some species they remain closed for years, opening only when heated, as during a forest fire.

The oldest living plants on earth belong in the genus *Pinus*. *P. longaeva* plants discovered in the White Mountains of California, U.S.A. are about 4,000 years old. Formerly this species was classified as *P. aristata* and even now some taxonomists treat *P. longaeva* as a subspecies of *P. aristata*.

The classification of the genus is still in much

19

dispute and there are, therefore, several systems in use. Because Krüssmann's *Manual of Cultivated Conifers* is used as guide for this book, we follow the classification of Krüssmann. He divides *Pinus* into 3 subgenera, and these into sections. The subgenus *Ducampopinus* (1) contains only the tropical *P. krempfii* from Vietnam. This very peculiar *Pinus* has needles to 5 mm wide. The subgenus *Haploxylon* (2) is divided into 3 sections. The section *Cembra* (a) contains several well-known species—*P. cembra, P. flexilis,* and *P. pumila.* The section *Strobus* (b) contains *P. monticola, P. parviflora, P. strobus, P. wallichiana,* etc. The third section in this subgenus is *Paracembra* (c) with, among others *P. aristata, P. bungeana, P. cembroides,* and *P. gerardiana.* The third subgenus is *Diploxylon* (3), subdivided into 8 sections. The most important of those are Section *Eupitys,* with *P. densiflora, P. leucodermis, P. nigra* and *P. sylvestris,* among others. In the Section *Banksia* are classified: *P. banksiana, P. contorta* and several subtropical species; in the Section *Pseudostrobus, P. jeffreyi, P. montezumae, P. ponderosa,* and a number of others.

Cultivars have derived from many species, among which are some of the most beautiful garden plants. Many of these cultivars have been found in the wild, although many have also originated in nurseries. Several cultivars, classified under *P. cembra,* belong to *P. pumila.* (Dendroflora #19, 1982)

A very beautiful plant for fairly large gardens is *P. leucodermis,* the Bosnian Pine. Some excellent cultivars come from this species, such as the dwarf form 'Compact Gem' and the very erect 'Satellit'.

Many garden forms derive from the European Mountain Pine, *P. mugo.* The pyramidal growing 'Rigi' is a beautiful form, with juvenile needles first grayish green and later dark green. The mountain form *P. mugo* var. *mughus* is widely planted, often as a groundcover. 'Mops' and 'Gnom' are *P. mugo* var. *mughus* clones which are superb in containers on balconies and in small gardens.

P. nigra, the Austrian Pine, is also widely planted. Some beautiful cultivars come from this species, among others the new 'Geant de Suisse'.

P. parviflora, found in Japan, is a fine, smaller tree. To it belong several garden forms, all with bluish gray needles. In Japan these cultivars are often used for bonsai cultivation. Some Dutch forms are 'Tempelhof' and 'Gimborn's Ideal'.

The Weymouth Pine, *P. strobus,* is not suitable for smaller gardens and is, moreover, sensitive to rust disease. The *P. strobus* cultivar 'Radiata' is the best known garden form, a low, broadly growing plant. In the United States the weeping form 'Pendula' is cultivated extensively. The Scotch Pine, *P. sylvestris,* is also very important in horticulture, particularly the

Pinus radiata. This species thrives in Ireland. (98)

cultivar 'Watereri'.

Pinus is a very important forestry tree. *P. sylvestris,* Scotch Pine, is planted in enormous quantities in plantations throughout Europe, even though it is not native to the coastal regions of western Europe. In the United States *P. contorta* is very important, especially on the west coast, as are *P. ponderosa* and *P. jeffreyi.* Cluster Pine, *P. pinaster,* is extensively planted in the coastal regions along the Atlantic Ocean and the Mediterranean seacoast, as is the Umbrella Pine, *P. pinea,* which bears adipose (fat containing) edible seeds.

Many species native to the mountain regions of Central America are not marginally hardy in the temperate latitudes. However, *P. cembroides* and *P. monophylla,* found in the dry, warm regions of southwestern North America, while rare in cultivation, are quite hardy. Incidentally, *P. monophylla* is the only species that appears to have one needle per fascicle. However, this needle is a connated double needle.

The Japanese equivalent of *P. nigra* is *P. thunbergii,* of which several cultivars are grown in Japan.

Until recently cultivars were grafted upon stocks to which they were closely related. Thus, cultivars with 5 needles per fascicle were always grafted upon 5-needled stock. Recently it has been found that this practice is not all that necessary. For instance, the grafts of 5-needled cultivars of *P. pumila* upon *P. contorta,* double needled, appear promising.

P. albicaulis	P. halepensis	P. pinaster
P. aristata	P. insularis	P. pinceana
P. aristata	P. jeffreyi	P. pinea
var. longaeva	P. khasya	P. pityusa
P. armandii	P. koraiensis	P. ponderosa
P. attenuata	P. krempfii	P. pringlei
P. ayacahuite	P. lambertiana	P. pseudostrobus
P. balfouriana	P. lawsonii	P. pumila
P. banksiana	P. leiophylla	P. pungens
P. brutia	P. leucodermis	P. quadrifolia
P. bungeana	P. lumholtzii	P. radiata
P. canariensis	P. massoniana	P. resinosa
P. caribaea	P. merkusii	P. rigida
P. cembra	P. michoacana	P. roxburghii
P. cembroides	P. monophylla	P. rzedowskii
P. chihuahuana	P. montezumae	P. sabiniana
P. clausa	P. monticola	P. serotina
P. contorta	P. morrisonicola	P. sibirica
P. coulteri	P. mugo	P. stankewiczii
P. culminicola	P. muricata	P. strobiformis
P. densiflora	P. nelsonii	P. strobus
P. douglasiana	P. nigra	P. sylvestris
P. echinata	P. oaxacana	P. tabuliformis
P. elliottii	P. occidentalis	P. taeda
P. engelmannii	P. oocarpa	P. taiwanensis
P. flexilis	P. palustris	P. teocote
P. gerardiana	P. parviflora	P. thunbergii
P. glabra	P. patula	P. washoensis
P. greggii	P. peuce	P. yunnanensis

Podocarpus/PODOCARPACEAE

The genus *Podocarpus* contains almost 100 species, the majority of which are not hardy in temperate latitudes. They are usually evergreen trees or shrubs, often with straight stems, although some species are shrub-like. The bark peels off in strips. The arrangement of the branches is often irregular. In this genus the shape of the leaves is quite varied, from small needlelike leaves, as in *P. nivalis,* to "leaf-like" as in *P. nagi* and *P. wallichiana.*

They are mono- or dioecious. The seeds with their solid husk look like drupes, due to the fleshy fruit or the colorful, fleshy, swollen "foot" on which they stand. The fruits remain green for some months, but on ripening turn purplish brown.

Recently, the botanical classification has been reworked by D. J. de Laubenfels. In the context of this book these interesting problems can be set aside, because so few are of importance in the European and North American garden. Most *Podocarpus* species are native to China, the islands of the southeastern Pacific Ocean and eastern Australia. A second concentration of *Podocarpus* is situated in southeastern Africa and a third in South America. In the south of Chile and Argentina an isolated distribution is also found.

P. alpinus is reasonably hardy in cool climates and forms a low, dense shrub. *P. lawrensis* becomes taller, but at present this species is viewed as a synonym for *P. alpinus.* This form is also quite hardy. *P. andinus* is

Podocarpus totara. Tropical splendor in an evening mood. Old trees in New Zealand.

sufficiently hardy to survive in Ireland and southern England.

P. dacrydioides is a superb tree, but is only useful in landscapes in very mild climates.

P. falcatus is a South African species from the Cape and Natal provinces, where it is an important forestry tree.

P. macrophyllus is often found in botanic collections. *P. nagi* is also in cultivation and is often planted in Japan.

P. nivalis is the hardiest species, originating in New Zealand, and forms a fairly low, very wide shrub with small fresh green needles and red "berries". The latter do not develop in Europe and North America because only one sex is in cultivation as the plants are propagated by cuttings. *P. totara* (a Maori name), native to New Zealand, is a gorgeous tree with a golden brown stem and short, sharp brownish green needles. It is only marginally hardy in temperate climates. The quite similar *P. acutifolius,* on the other hand, is hardy, but does not develop into a tree but remains shrub-like.

In tropical regions several species are used in forestry.

P. acutifolius	P. ensiculus
P. affinis	P. falcatus
P. alpinus	P. ferrugineus
(incl. P. lawrencii)	P. ferruginoides
P. amarus	P. fleuryi
P. andinus	P. formosensis
P. angustifolius	P. forrestii
P. annamensis	P. gibbsii
P. archboldii	P. glaucus
P. aristulatus	P. glomeratus
P. brassii	P. gnidioides
P. brevifolius	P. gracilior
P. buchii	P. guatemalensis
P. cardenasii	P. hallii
P. cinctus	P. harmsianus
P. compactus	P. henkelii
P. comptonii	P. idenburgensis
P. coriaceus	P. imbricatus
P. costalis	P. koordersii
P. cumingii	P. ladei
P. curvifolius	P. lambertii
P. dacrydioides	P. latifolius
P. decipiens	P. ledermannii
P. decumbens	P. leonii
P. deflexus	P. longifoliolatus
P. dispermus	P. lucienii
P. distichus	P. macrophyllus
P. drouynianus	P. madagascariensis
P. ekmanii	P. magnifolius
P. elatus	P. mannii
P. elongatus	P. matudai

P. milanjianus	P. pittieri	P. sprucei
P. minor	P. polystachus	P. standleyi
P. montanus	P. purdieanus	P. steupii
P. motleyi	P. reichei	P. steyermarkii
P. nagi	P. roraimae	P. tepuiensis
P. neriifolius	P. rospigliosii	P. thevetiifolius
P. nivalis	P. rostratus	P. totara
P. novae-caledoniae	P. rumphii	P. urbanii
P. nubigenus	P. salignus	P. ustus
P. oleifolius	P. salomoniensis	P. utilior
P. pallidus	P. selloi	P. victorianus
P. pendulifolius	P. silvestris	P. viellardii
P. philippinensis	P. spicatus	P. vitiensis
P. pilgeri	P. spinulosus	P. wallichianus

Pseudolarix/PINACEAE

Pseudolarix, also called Golden Larch for its beautiful fall color, is a monotypic genus. The branches are arranged horizontally; the deciduous leaves are soft and light green, needlelike and arranged in fascicles, as in *Larix* and *Cedrus*. The cones are ovate, 5–7 cm long and ripen the first year. The cone scales are rhombic (diamond-shaped) and somewhat fleshy. The small seeds are winged and usually germinate slowly.

P. amabilis (*P. kaempferi*) grows to about 15 m tall in cooler latitudes but in its native habitat, eastern China, much taller. Fortune introduced this beautiful tree into England in 1852. *P. amabilis* is entirely hardy. Beautiful specimens can be seen in the Gimborn Arboretum, Doorn and in Pinetum Blijdenstein in Hilversum. Despite it hardiness, *P. amabilis* is relatively rare, because the seeds often do not germinate.

P. amabilis (*P. kaempferi*)

Pseudotaxus/TAXACEAE

Pseudotaxus is a monotypic genus, found in China in the province of Zhejiang.

P. chienii looks in many ways like *Taxus*, but differs from other *Taxaceae* in that the papillae located on the underside of the needles are lacking.

The plant is dioecious and has hard seeds surrounded by a white fleshy seed coat.

P. chienii was discovered about 1930 in the forests near Lungtsun, Zhejiang and was originally classified under *Taxus*. The species is not in cultivation in the West.

P. chienii (= *Nothotaxus chienii*)

Pseudotsuga/PINACEAE

At least 5 species are known of the genus *Pseudotsuga*, but depending upon the botanist up to 20. Superficially they look much like spruce (*Picea*), differing largely in the form of the cones.

They are tall trees. The branches are arranged irregularly radially. The needles are much like those of *Picea* and *Abies*; at first glance they can easily be confused.

Pseudotsuga is monoecious; the male "flowers" are axillary, cone-shaped and covered with short-stemmed stamens. The female "flowers" are terminal, on short shoots. The cones are pendulous, as in *Picea*, ripening in the first year. The seed scales protrude from the cones.

The 5 generally accepted species are found in North America, China and Japan.

P. japonica is rarely found in cultivation, though reasonably hardy. It becomes about 25 m tall.

P. macrocarpa from southern California is not consistently hardy in colder latitudes. The cones are much larger than those of the other species, hence the name *macrocarpa*.

By far the best known and most important species is *P. menziesii,* the Douglas Fir. This tree was introduced into England in 1827 by Douglas and hence the common name. However, Menzies, a Scottish naturalist, first discovered this tree in 1791 in British Columbia, Canada, so it is named in his honor. The smaller form with grayish green needles, found growing in the mountains, is sometimes classified as the variety *glauca*. Specimens in Oregon and Washington, U.S.A., where *P. menziesii* is the most

Pseudotsuga menziesii 'Pendula'. Old tree. This weeping form is rare. (3)

abundant conifer, grow 60–80 m tall.

P. sinensis, from China, is not hardy in cooler climates, often suffering from late night frosts. The related species *P. wilsoniana* is also very rare in cultivation.

A few cultivars have been derived from *P. menziesii.* 'Fletcheri' is fairly common. It is a creeping form with grayish green needles, suitable for large rock gardens. Other forms include 'Pendula', a weeping form. The landscape value of these cultivars is unjustifiably limited. The species itself is much too large for use in gardens. Douglas Fir is a very important forestry tree.

P. japonica	*P. sinensis*
P. macrocarpa	*P. wilsoniana*
P. menziesii	

Saxogothea/PODOCARPACEAE

Saxegothea is a monotypic genus. It is a small evergreen tree, superficially looking like *Taxus,* but with a totally different cone, which is round and thick composed of fleshy, thickened seed lobes. It is native to Patagonia in southern Chile, where it forms forests. This species is reasonably hardy; offspring from cuttings are in cultivation in the Netherlands, and can be grown in sheltered sites in colder latitudes.

The name is derived from Prince Albert van Sachsen-Coburg, Gotha, the husband of Queen Victoria.

A beautiful specimen, many meters tall and broad, is in the Arboretum Killerton, in southwestern England.

S. conspicua

Sciadopitys/PINACEAE

The genus *Sciadopitys* includes only one species, *S. verticillata*. It is an evergreen tree with a cone-shaped crown, often irregularly shaped. The leaves are double needles that grow together on the "long" side. They are arranged like little umbrellas at the end of the year's shoots. The tree is monoecious; the cones are ovate and ripen in the second year.

The species is native to Japan on the islands of Honshu, Shikoku and Kyushu. *S. verticillata* is cultivated in large numbers in Europe and North America as the plant is quite hardy. Beautiful specimens can be admired in the Arboretum Von Gimborn, Doorn.

S. verticillata prefers a clayey soil. In slightly acid soil the plants sometimes turn yellow.

Several cultivars are grown including 'Aurea' with

golden yellow needles, and 'Pendula', a weeping form. Neither is commonly found in gardens and parks.

S. verticillata

Sequoia/TAXODIACEAE

Redwood, *Sequoia sempervirens,* is the only species in the genus *Sequoia.* It is an evergreen tree; the bark can become 20–30 cm thick. The leaves look much like *Taxus* needles. The young shoots, however, branch entirely differently. The cones are small, 2–3 cm long, ovate and ripen in the second year. *S. sempervirens* is the tallest conifer in the world. The tallest deciduous tree is *Eucalyptus amygdalina,* which can become slightly taller. Several *S. sempervirens* have been located reaching more than 120 m. The cir-diameter of the trunk is immense, reaching more than 6 m. They can live for more than 3,000 years.

The Redwoods grow in the coastal region of northern California, U.S.A., where humidity is very high. In the forests, there is a daily mist that lifts only in the course of the day. Under these ideal conditions the trees grow rapidly. There is a marked route from Crescent City on the coast leading to San Francisco called the Avenue of Giants. This trip makes an unforgettable impression on visitors. While this route has become a tourist attraction in typical American fashion, it does not alter the fact that one is overwhelmed by the grandeur of these forests. Some of the forms of the trees are quite fantastic. The chimney tree is open the length of the trunk, like a chimney, but grows on quite unperturbed. There is also the One Log Shop, a store in a fallen, hollow trunk. In addition, there is a tree through which you can drive a car.

In the U.S. National and California State Parks nothing may be cut down or cleared away, not even fallen trees, a form of management that is leading to grave problems.

In its habitat *S. sempervirens* is widely planted for the production of timber. The trees can be cut in 80 years, and supply enormous quantities of light, indestructible and easily processed lumber. Outside its natural habitat, Redwood supplies considerably less timber.

In cooler climates *S. sempervirens* is not hardy. Passable specimens are growing in the Arboretum Trompenburg, Rotterdam and in the Arboretum of the University of Agriculture in Wageningen. A large tree, of at least 35 m, can be found on the bank of Lake Geneva, in a public garden in Lausanne, Switzerland.

Sequoia sempervirens and *Sequoiadendron giganteum* in the Stourhead Garden, England. (117)

A few cultivars have been developed. 'Adpressa' grows irregularly, is reasonably hardy, and is a dwarfish shrub-like tree, with silver-white growing tips; the leaves are more closely arranged than those of the species. A true dwarf form is 'Prostrata', with short, wide needles, but it is unfortunately quite tender.

S. sempervirens

Sequoiadendron/TAXODIACEAE

Like its close relative, *Sequoia sempervirens,* *Sequoiadendron* is a monotypic genus. In the United States the popular name is Big Tree or Mammoth Tree. This widely grown tree grows to about 100 m in its natural habitat, but in Europe a height of 50 m is rare. The circumference of the trunk is as large or larger than that of *S. sempervirens. S. giganteum* also becomes extremely old; trees of 3,000–3,500 years are known; most are, however, 400–1500 years old. Therefore, they are among the oldest living trees in the world. The largest specimen ever found in Calaveras National Forest was 135 m, a second tree measured 114 m. These trees no longer survive. The average height is now 8–100 m. The so-called "General Sherman" is 83 m, the diameter of the trunk is 11 m, the age 3,500 years. The "General Grant" is a little taller and 12 m wide.

Sequoiadendrons are found in the Sierra Nevada mountains of California, at an elevation of 1,500–2,000 m, some 50–100 miles east of the coastal region where *Sequoia* grows.

The bark is spongy, very thick, and nearly incombustible. As a consequence, these trees are able to survive forest fires. The needles look much like those of *Cryptomeria* but are shorter. The tree is monoecious. Cones develop on very young trees; they are cylindrical and remain on the tree for many years.

Sequoiadendron was discovered only 150 years ago. It is not certain who introduced it into England. John Bidwell discovered it near the Sacramento River. He did not study the tree nor did he announce his discovery. In 1852 the tree was re-discovered by A. T. Dowd, who was following a wounded bear. He mentioned his discovery to Lobb, who was working for the firm of J. Veitch & Sons, Exeter, England, as a plant-hunter. Lobb sent a large quantity of seeds to England from which thousands of trees were cultivated. John D. Matthew, who traveled in California at the same time, sent seeds to Scotland, which arrived before those of Lobb. We can assume that the oldest *S. giganteum* in Scotland are descended from these seeds. Therefore, the trees on European continent can hardly be older than 110 years, notwithstanding their huge dimensions.

Several cultivars have been selected, of which 'Pendulum' is the best known. This weeping tree often develops bizarre habits of growth. This form is fairly common in warmer latitudes but in unfavorable climates becomes quite ugly. 'Glaucum' grows erect, with pyramidal form and has a steel-blue color. Another dwarf form is 'Pygmaeum' which grows very slowly and compactly.

S. giganteum

Taiwania/TAXODIACEAE

The genus *Taiwania* contains 2 species, both are tall, evergreen trees. The leaves are needlelike and look much like those of *Cryptomeria*. *Taiwania* is dioecious; the cones differ from those of *Cryptomeria* in possessing 2 seeds on each seed scale while *Cryptomeria* always has 3.

T. cryptomerioides is moderately hardy in England, the European coastal regions and southern North America. Its natural habitat is in the mountains of

Taiwan, where the tree was discovered in 1904 by Konishi.

T. flousiana was recently discovered in China in the basin of the Salween River near Upper Burma. It differs only slightly from *T. cryptomerioides* and these differences are probably insufficient to maintain it as a separate species.

T. cryptomerioides
T. flousiana

Taxodium/TAXODIACEAE

Taxodium is a genus containing 3 species. Two of the 3 species are deciduous, the third is more or less evergreen. All species develop into large trees; in Europe they sometimes reach 40 m. *Taxodium* species are usually found growing in swampy sites or also in shallow water. All form respiratory roots or "knees," a form of aerial roots around the stem, that are sometimes several meters removed from it when older.

Taxodium is monoecious, the cones are short-stemmed, round to ovate and burst open on ripening. The leaves are needlelike and arranged in 2 rows on

Taxodium distichum. Here in its natural habitat in Georgia, U.S.A. along the Alatamaha River.

10–15 cm long shoots that fall off with the leaves. The soft green needles are 1–2 cm long and turn a beautiful bronze in the fall. The bark of *Taxodium* is usually thin and smooth.

T. distichum, the Swamp Cypress, is by far the best known of this genus. It is native to southeastern U.S.A., mainly Florida and Alabama. Beautiful and very large specimens can be found in the Everglades National Park in Florida. *T. distichum* is very common in cultivation, growing best in damp to wet habitats.

A cultivar of *T. distichum* is 'Pendens', a tall tree with a cone-shaped, dense crown. The twigs are somewhat pendulous. A beautiful lane with 50-year old trees is located near the railway station in Boskoop, the Netherlands.

T. ascendens is much shorter than *T. distichum*, rarely reaching a height of more than 15 m. The trunk differs from *T. distichum* in the thick bark and the thickened base. The needles are appressed against the short shoots and more awl-shaped. This species is found in Alabama, Virginia and Florida. *T. ascendens* is no longer viewed as species, but as a variety of *T. distichum* by some botanists. However, the tree differs sufficiently morphologically that this opinion is not shared here. The cultivar 'Nutans' is smaller, more columnar, but has a broad base. The twigs are first appressed, later geniculate. The cultivar is much more common than the species.

T. mucronatum is a Mexican species that is hardly grown outside North America. This species is usually evergreen, but otherwise is much like *T. distichum*. However, the branches stand off more. The needles and their short shoots drop off only in the second year.

A gigantic specimen of *T. mucronatum* can be found in Santa Maria del Tule, not far from the city of Oaxaca, Mexico. This tree is about 40 m tall with a crown circumference of 61 m. This tree was formerly thought to be extremely old. Recent thought, after careful measurements of the extremely irregular trunk, is that the tree consists of several specimens growing together, and that it is barely 1000 years old. (Mitt. Duetsche Dendr. Gesellschaft 1939, pages 64–72)

T. ascendens
T. distichum
T. mucronatum

Taxus/TAXACEAE

The genus *Taxus* contains 7 or 8 species, or in another view, is only one very variable species, with a series of subspecies that can be considered as geographical varieties. They are trees or shrubs, with reddish brown stems. The bark peels in rolls off old stems. The needles remain on the plants for some time, up to 8 years. They are usually somewhat arched, dark green and arranged in two rows.

The plants are dioecious. The male "flowers" emerge as small spikes in the leaf axils. The female "flowers" emerge at the end of the side shoots, that is to say, the ovule is located in the axil of the upper scale. The seeds are ovate and pressed, and enclosed in a fleshy, red seed coat. The needles contain a poison which is deadly, even in small quantities, especially for hoofed animals. The seeds are also poisonous; the fleshy seed coat is not.

T. baccata is native to all of Europe with the exception of the Scandinavian countries and the coastal regions, Asia Minor, the Caucasus mountains and North Africa. In the Netherlands it was wiped out in the Middle Ages but brought back into cultivation within living memory. Usually they grow into small trees. When they can develop freely, they grow to 20 m tall and at least as wide. They can become very old.

T. baccata is easily pruned into all sorts of shapes. In the Baroque Era and later, the most bizarre topiaries were made from *Taxus*. As a hedge plant, *T. baccata* is of the utmost utility as they can be formed into very tight, narrow, dense hedges.

In the course of the centuries many garden forms have been developed. They are not always easy to identify, since much cross breeding of cultivars has also occurred. One of the best known forms is the Irish *Taxus*, *T. baccata* 'Fastigiata', widely planted in cemeteries. *T. baccata* 'Repandens' is a very useful, practical and beautiful ground cover. One can also find various yellow-needled and yellow variegated

Taxus baccata. A 'lane' of topiaries in France (Nogent-sur-Vernisson).

cultivars, such as 'Standishii', columnar; 'Fastigiata Aurea', a variegated columnar; 'Washingtonii' a wide, bushy shrub; and 'Summergold', a beautiful variegated low shrub.

Various forms with aberrant needle forms are also known, e.g. *T. baccata* 'Adpressa' and 'Adpressa Aurea'. A markedly different form is 'Amersfoort', delivered to a hospital in Amersfoort, the Netherlands, in 1939 by the nurseryman Van den Hoorn from Boskoop. For years the plant was considered to be a *Podocarpus*. Only recently, based on careful scientific analysis, was its correct identity learned.

In northern Germany the so-called Aprather types are widely planted. They all have a wide, shrub-like habit — e.g. 'Praesident', 'Corona', 'Kadett'. From 'Fastigiata' many good columnar forms have been selected that have come into the market under a variety of names.

T. canadensis is found in the eastern part of North America, but is of little ornamental value. The very hardy *T. cuspidata* is highly valued in America, but little planted elsewhere. The cultivar 'Nana', on the other hand, is very common.

Via the hybrid *T. × media,* originating from the crossing *T. baccata × T. cuspidata,* a long series of good cultivars have been selected. They were mainly propagated and sold in America. The very best of this series is *T. × media* 'Hicksii', an excellent form for hedges. An exceptionally beautiful columnar is 'Stricta Viridis', surprisingly only rarely available.

Taxus is unsuitable for forestry. Small items are made out of the tough and durable wood.

T. baccata
T. brevifolia
T. canadensis
T. celebica
T. cuspidata
T. floridana
T. globosa
T. wallichiana

Tetraclinis/CUPRESSACEAE

Tetraclinis is a monotypic genus, related to *Callitris* and *Widdringtonia*. The twigs, however, look like *Thuja*. It becomes a moderately tall tree, and is native to North Africa, Malta, and an isolated stand in southeastern Spain.

It is a very valuable evergreen tree for warm, dry habitats. *Tetraclinis* is not at all hardy in northerly latitudes. The resin is used as an ingredient in varnish.

T. articulata

Thuja plicata. The giant Tree of Life. Natural habitat in western North America. Here the 'Champion' in the Olympic National Park, Washington U.S.A.

Thuja/CUPRESSACEAE

The genus *Thuja* contains 6 species native to North America and southeast Asia. They are evergreen trees, exceptionally also shrubs. They have a fairly slender habit and often form cone-shaped crowns. The twigs are flat, the leaves overlapping and scale-like, looking much like those of *Chamaecyparis* and *Calocedrus*.

Thuja is monoecious, the male "flowers" are small and terminal, the female "flowers" are ovate to oblong, singular and very small. The cones are about 1 cm long, ovate, with leathery scales and a hook-like projection on the back of the scales.

The best known and most widely cultivated *Thuja* is *T. occidentalis*, the western Tree of Life (Arborvitae), native to the eastern United States on swampy sites. *T. occidentalis* has been grown in Europe for centuries and in the course of the years many cultivars have been developed. *T. occidentalis* is a superb plant for hedges. They do not tolerate salt spray nearly as well as *Cupressocyparis*. *T. occidentalis* develops into a slender tree to a maximum height of 20 m. The cultivars do not become nearly as tall. There are several columnar cultivars, such as 'Pyramidalis Compacta' and 'Columna'; the latter is especially widely cultivated in Germany. The somewhat wider

27

growing 'Rosenthalii' and the slender 'Malonyana' are valuable. There are several globose cultivars, such as 'Little Champion' and 'Woodwardii'. In addition, there are yellow-needled cultivars, such as the excellent 'Sunkist' and the globose 'Golden Globe'; the white variegated 'Beaufort' is especially striking.

The eastern Tree of Life, *T. orientalis* is much less hardy and much smaller. The cones are larger than those of *T. occidentalis*. The cultivar 'Aurea Nana' is a very dense, thick, slow growing yellow columnar form. It is valuable and quite hardy. The beautiful, tall growing sulfur yellow 'Elegantissima' is widely cultivated in France and Italy.

T. plicata, the giant Tree of Life, is native to western North America where it reaches heights of 40–50 m, as it can in cultivation. Old trees often have thick, heavily drooping branches on which roots form spontaneously when coming in contact with the earth, from which new trunks grow. A single individual can grow this way into a true 'forest'. Several cultivars have been developed from *T. plicata*. *T. plicata* 'Atrovirens' is used on a large scale in France as a hedge plant. 'Zebrina' is a nicely variegated columnar tree.

T. standishii is native to Japan. In its native habitat it grows to 30 m high but is only a small tree in cultivation. This species is quite rare in Europe and North America, but deserves wider usage. Closely related is *T. koraiensis*, just as beautiful, but even rarer.

T. plicata forms large forest stands in its habitat and has been planted experimentally, particularly in Germany where good stands are now growing. The wood is light, strong, resists decay and is easily processed. The North American Indians used this wood for totem poles, canoes and long houses.

> *T. koraiensis*
> *T. occidentalis*
> *T. orientalis*
> *T. plicata*
> *T. standishii*
> *T. sutchuenensis*

Thujopsis/CUPRESSACEAE

A monotypic genus, forming small trees to about 20 m tall in its natural habitat, Japan. In colder climates *Thujopis* barely becomes a tree, usually becoming a wide, pyramidal shrub. The twigs are irregularly arranged, the leaves are coarse and scale-like, much coarser than in *Thuja*. The cones are wide ovate, 12–15 mm long.

The variety *T. dolobrata* var. *hondai* forms a good

stem easier than the species itself. The leaves of this variety are somewhat darker green and also somewhat smaller. The well-known cultivar 'Variegata', with white variegated scales, almost always grows shrub-like. The beautiful 'Nana' is a small low globe, suitable for rock gardens.

All *Thujopsis* are completely hardy and should be more widely planted.

> *T. dolobrata*

Torreya/TAXACEAE

Six species in the genus *Torreya* are known, all relatively rare in European cultivation. They are evergreen trees with a rough bark and radially arranged branches. In cooler climates *Torreya* species usually remain shrub-like. The leaves are needlelike, fairly long, 3–6 cm, stiff and pointed. The needles of *Cephalotaxus*, which look the same, are not sharp.

Torreya is dioecious; the seeds are ovate, 5 cm long, with a thin wooden coat surrounded by a thick fleshy seed coat. They ripen in the second year.

T. californica, native to California, U.S.A., is by far the best known species. Its dark green, long needles are easily confused with the similar *T. nucifera* from China. Young plants without fruits are hardly distinguishable from one another. *T. grandis* has shorter and duller needles, and sometimes develops into a small tree in cool climates.

> *T. californica*
> *T. fargesii*
> *T. grandis*
> *T. jackii*
> *T. nucifera*
> *T. taxifolia*

Tsuga/PINACEAE

The genus *Tsuga* contains about 18 species, native to the temperate regions of North America, Japan and China. They are fairly tall trees, always evergreen. The buds are very small, the needles quite short and somewhat overlapping. *Tsuga* is monoecious, the "flowers" of both sexes are very small. The cones are also small, 1–2 cm long, but formed in large numbers. They ripen the first year, but usually stay on the tree 2 years.

The botanical classification is simple, containing only 2 sections. The section *Micropeuce* (1) includes all species, except 3. The section *Hesperopeuce* (2) contains the remaining 3—*T. crassifolia*, the Chinese *T. longibracteata*, and *T. mertensiana*. The best known *Tsuga* is *T. canadensis*, Canadian Hemlock. It is a tall, densely branched tree to 25 m tall, found in eastern Canada and the United States as far south as the Carolinas and Alabama. This species develops best in a damp and cool climate so is not suitable in continental climates. *T. canadensis* is often planted in parks and public gardens. In the course of the years many cultivars have been developed. The best known is *T. canadensis* 'Pendula', a wide, weeping form, that does not grow into a tree because it does not form a terminal. Monumental specimens can be found. Not all plants bearing the name 'Pendula' belong to the same clone, so the name 'Pendula' must be treated with some care; it is actually more a collective name such as in *Picea abies* 'Pendula' and *Chamaecyparis nootkatensis* 'Pendula'. In addition to the weeping forms there are a large number of dwarf and creeping forms, e.g. 'Jeddeloh' and 'Cole'.

A second important species is *T. heterophylla*, which is of great importance in forestry on the west coast of the United States and Canada. *T. heterophylla* grows fast, but requires a high humidity to flourish—even more than *T. canadensis*. They grow to more than 60 m. This species is less frequently planted in Europe than *T. canadensis*.

T. mertensiana is found in the coastal mountains of North America paralleling the Pacific Ocean. This species is much smaller, in the most favorable conditions only about 20 m, usually much lower, and in Europe hardly taller than 10–12 m. It is a beautiful conifer, but unfortunately rarely planted. It is not only fussy as to site, but is also difficult to propagate.

The cultivar *T. mertensiana* 'Blue Star' has grayish blue needles and is smaller than the species. The Japanese *T. sieboldiana* is another fine, but rare, tree with dark green needles. The underside of the needles is conspicuously silver-white.

All the remaining *Tsuga* species are rarely seen in collections, in part because they are not in cultivation.

T. blaringhemii	*T. diversifolia*	*T. longibracteata*
T. calcarea	*T. dumosa*	*T. mertensiana*
T. canadensis	*T. formosana*	*T. patens*
T. caroliniana	*T. forrestii*	*T. sieboldii*
T. chinensis	*T. heterophylla*	*T. tschekiangensis*
T. crassifolia	*T. × jeffreyi*	*T. yunnanensis*

Widdringtonia/CUPRESSACEAE

Three species are now assigned to this genus while earlier 5–6 were. Some have recently been brought into synonymy with *W. schwarzii*. All are native to South Africa.

They are small to medium tall trees, evergreen and with a fairly narrow, ascending habit. They are related to *Callitris* but differ in their smaller leaves, which are arranged in pairs and usually scale-like. The juvenile leaves are needlelike, as in *Thuja* and *Chamaecyparis*.

Widdringtonia is monoecious; the cones are ovate to globular, 1–3 cm thick, with four woody valves that burst open on maturity.

The species of *Widdringtonia* are only suitable for very mild climates. Most specimens in cooler climates are grown in greenhouses.

W. cedarbergensis
W. cupressoides
W. schwarzii

Tsuga mertensiana. Forms forests in Oregon and Washington, U.S.A., at elevations above 1500 m. In Europe it is fairly difficult to grow. Here a tree near Crater Lake, a lake 10 km in diameter formed by rainfall in an old volcanic crater.

Abies alba. Native to all mountainous regions in all of Central Europe. Very valuable for timber; occasionally planted as an ornamental tree. (35)

Abies alba 'Compacta'. A rare dwarf form, on the market since 1885. (71)

Abies alba 'Pyramidalis'. As a young plant, growth columnar; when mature the habit is more conical. (61)

Abies alba 'Pendula'. Fairly tall weeping form.

31

Abies amabilis 'Spreading Star'. This low growing form originated years ago in the Pinetum Blijdenstein, Hilversum, The Netherlands. Younger plants practically creep. (3)

Abies × arnoldiana 'Poulsen'. A hybrid between *A. koreana* and *A. veitchii*. Poulsen repeated this cross and obtained plants that grow faster than *A. koreana* and also bear longer needles. The purplish blue cones are formed when this twin is quite young. (61)

Abies balsamea 'Nana'. About 15 cultivars of this species are known. The dwarf form pictured is the best known. Very suitable for rock gardens. (1)

Abies bracteata. One of the few
Abies species with sharp
needles. (116)

Abies bracteata. Cone of an old
tree.

Abies cephalonica. Cones. The
Greek Silver Spruce is native
to Greece and some islands in
the Aegean Sea.

Abies cephalonica 'Meyer's
Dwarf'. A relatively new, low
growing dwarf form. The habit
is somewhat irregular. Suitable
for rock gardens. (1)

Abies concolor. Cones. The well-known Colorado Fir is frequently used in larger gardens and parks. It is native to the Western part of North America. The tree is completely hardy and grows fairly fast in Europe.

Abies concolor 'Archer's Dwarf'. A rare dwarf form originating in the U.S.A. Suitable for rock gardens. (1)

Abies concolor 'Compacta'. Well-known dwarf form of the Colorado Fir; irregular habit. Suitable for the rock garden. (1)

Abies concolor 'Gable's Weeping'. A rare creeping form; sometimes the branches ascend slightly. Slow growing. For collectors of dwarf conifers. (1)

Abies concolor var. *lowiana*. This variety is widely distributed in the Sierra Nevada Mountains of western North America. The tree grows bolt upright often to 70 m tall. In Europe this species is quite rare and sometimes considered as a separate species, *A. lowiana*. Here *A. concolor* var. *lowiana* grows together with *Betula fontinalis* in its natural environment at 3000 m elevation.

Abies concolor 'Piggelmee'. Witches'-broom from *A. concolor*, originating in the Netherlands; propagated by grafting. (38)

Abies concolor 'Violacea'. This tree has beautiful grayish blue needles; quite rare in nurseries. Beautiful, old specimens can be found in some parks. (2)

Abies concolor 'Wattezii'. Slow growing form with pale yellow, later silvery white, needles. Discovered as a mutation around 1900 in the Wattez nursery in the Netherlands. (5)

Abies concolor 'Wattezii Prostrata'. The needles of this creeping form resemble the preceding. Probably originated through grafting of side shoots which then remained stable. (38)

Abies concolor 'Wintergold'. A new, yellow-needled form of *A. concolor*. This form was selected from seedlings around 1959 by G. Horstmann, Schneverdingen, BRD (Federal Republic of Germany). Not yet widely for sale. (63)

Abies delavayi 'Herdford'. Rare dwarf form; developed in the USA.

36

Abies delavayi var. *georgei*. Tall tree, with long dark green needles, native to Yunnan Province, China. It is questionable if the true species is in cultivation. It is a fine tree for the medium-large garden. (81)

Abies delavayi var. *georgei*. Male and female inflorescences.

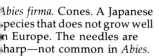

Abies firma. Cones. A Japanese species that does not grow well in Europe. The needles are sharp—not common in *Abies.*

Abies fraseri. This species, related to *A. balsamea,* has its natural distribution in the Allegheny Mountains of the U.S.A. Photographed here in the Grandfather Mountains with an undergrowth of *Vaccinium.*

37

Abies grandis. This species is native to western North America and is forested in Europe. (26)

Abies homolepis. A very beautiful Japanese species that becomes a fairly tall tree. It is completely hardy and deserves more attention; can be propagated from seeds. (61)

Abies homolepis. Cones.

Abies homolepis. Female inflorescences.

Abies homolepis. A handsome dwarf form, not yet named; originating in West Germany. (62)

Abies homolepis. A yet unnamed creeping form that certainly deserves more attention. (1)

Abies koreana 'Aurea'. Slow growing yellow-needled form suitable for small gardens; still rare. (62)

Abies koreana 'Compact Dwarf'. A broadly spreading semi-dwarf form. At times that a terminal branch develops the spreading habit is lost. (62)

Abies koreana. Korean Silver Fir.
Universally grown; a small tree
very suitable for smaller
gardens. Often bears beautiful,
bluish purple cones at an early
age. (35)

Abies koreana. Male and female
inflorescences. (1)

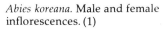

Abies koreana. Cones. (1)

Abies koreana 'Horstmann's Silberlocke'. The needles of this small tree are twisted around their axis so that the silvery white back is clearly visible. (1)

Abies koreana 'Piccolo'. Older plant; peculiar short-needled, broadly growing garden form. (1)

Abies lasiocarpa 'Compacta'. Widely grown dwarf form with bluish grey needles; suitable for larger rock gardens. (6)

41

Abies magnifica. North
American species found in
the mountain regions of
California. Fairly rare in
Europe. (21)

Abies magnifica 'Nana'. A rare
dwarf form of unknown origin.
(1)

Abies nordmanniana. Cones.
This well-known species is native to the Caucasus; often
planted in larger gardens.

Abies nordmanniana 'Golden Spreader'. Small, slow-growing form, very suitable for the rock garden. The golden-yellow needles sometimes burn in warm and dry summers. (82)

Abies numidica 'Pendula'. Recumbent form; fairly rare in cultivation. (1)

Abies pinsapo. The Spanish Silver Spruce. Solitary tree in the Ronda Mountains, South Spain. The needles of this handsome species are always arranged radially (not in two rows).

Abies pinsapo 'Aurea'. Slow growing; needles are sulfur-yellow. Not fully hardy in northerly latitudes. (17)

Abies pinsapo 'Glauca'. Well-known blue-needled form. A valuable tree for smaller gardens. (61)

Abies pinsapo 'Horstmann'. Witches'-broom from A. pinsapo 'Glauca'. Suitable for the rock garden. (1)

Abies pinsapo. 'Kelleriis'. Very hardy Danish form; fast growing. Young plants often very irregularly shaped. (83)

Abies pinsapo. Growing in its natural distribution area in the south of Spain; dwarf form.

Abies procera and *Pinus lambertiana*. Growing together in their native habitat in Yosemite National Park, California, U.S.A.

Abies procera 'Glauca'. Cones.

Abies procera 'Blaue Hexe'. A fine new dwarf form originating in Germany. This attractive plant deserves more attention. (62)

Abies squamata. This Chinese species cannot be confused with any other *Abies*-species because of the unique bark.

Abies spectabilis. A rare species; photographed in Nepal on the Milke Danda Range. Rarely cultivated.

Acmopyle pancheri. Silver colored stoma on both the under and upper sides of the needles. Native to New Caledonia. (21)

Abies veitchii 'Pendula'. Beautiful weeping tree, rarely seen in cultivation. The name is probably not validly published. (8)

Abies veitchii. Detail of the trunk; typical of this species.

Actinostrobus pyramidalis. Cone berries and scale-like leaves.

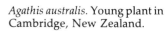

Agathis australis. The Australian Kauri Fir. Human scale contrasted with this gigantic tree; photographed on the northern peninsula of New Zealand's subtropical North Island.

Agathis australis. Young plant in Cambridge, New Zealand.

Agathis australis. The cone resembles that of *Araucaria.* The leaves have a broad blade and do not look at all like a conifer.

Agathis dammara. Young plant cultivated in a greenhouse. (3)

Agathis robusta. Photograph of the bark of a tree in a Brisbane, Australia park. Mrs. van Hoey Smith.

Amentotaxus argotaenia.

Araucaria balansae. Native to New Caledonia and becomes a small tree in subtropical regions. Rare in cultivation. (49)

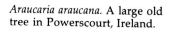
Araucaria araucana. A large old
tree in Powerscourt, Ireland.

Araucaria araucana. The base
of the trunk looks like an
elephant's foot.

Araucaria araucana. Cones.

Araucaria araucana. Male
inflorescence.

Araucaria columnaris (right), and *A. heterophylla* (left). Rare species from New Caledonia. *A. columnaris* differs from the better known *A. heterophylla* in the compact, less 'feather-like' habit. (48)

Araucaria cunninghamii. Native to New Guinea and northern Australia. This tree was photographed in its natural distribution area.

Araucaria cunninghamii. Cone.

51

Araucaria heterophylla. The well-known Norfolk Pine; better known as "*A. excelsa.*" The tree becomes more than 50m tall and is often planted in tropical regions. Shown here with *Populus nigra* 'Italica'. (92)

Araucaria heterophylla. Detail o the cone.

Athrotaxis cupressoides. Resembles *Cryptomeria;* native t Australia and Tasmania. Here growing in the wild near Pine Lake, Tasmania.

Araucaria rulei. This species is native to New Caledonia; very rare in cultivation.

Athrotaxis cupressoides. The tree bears abundant cones.

Athrotaxis laxifolia. Large tree in a Scottish garden. Although native to Tasmania, this species is slightly hardier than *A. cupressoides.* (33)

Athrotaxis laxifolia. Cones.

Athrotaxis selaginoides. Cones.
Native to Tasmania.

Austrocedrus chilensis and
Calocedrus decurrens.
Austrocedrus is a rare species
from the Andes mountains;
reasonably hardy. (21)

Austrocedrus chilensis. Terminal
branch of a young tree. The
shape of the scales can hardly
be confused with those of any
other species. (1)

Callitris columellaris. Small Australian tree; only rarely found in cultivation. (93)

Callitris columellaris. Branch with 2 cones.

Callitris rhomboidea. Branch with cones.

Callitris rhomboidea and *Araucaria heterophylla.* Large trees native to Tasmania. (94)

Calocedrus decurrens. This species is better known as *Libocedrus decurrens.* Native to western North America; the tree grows columnar in its northern distribution area and more conical in the southern part. (26)

Calocedrus decurrens. Branch with male inflorescences.

Calocedrus decurrens. Tree with witches'-broom; in its natural habitat, near Bear Basin, Oregon, USA.

Calocedrus decurrens. Branch
with typical cones, by which
Calocedrus can always be distinguished.

Calocedrus decurrens
'Compacta'. Compact growing
form. The original plant is still
alive in the Westonbirt
Arboretum, England. (1)

Calocedrus decurrens
'Aureovariegata'. Yellow twigs
can be seen scattered over the
entire tree. These yellow twigs
are more abundant in a warm
climate than in colder regions.
(43)

Calocedrus decurrens 'Intricata'. Rather rare dwarf form, selected from seedlings in 1938 by Noble, USA. The winter color is brownish green. (28)

Cedrus atlantica. Trees in their natural habitat near Ifrane in the middle Atlas Mountains in Morocco, growing together with *Quercus ilex*. The Atlas Cedars in nature often display bluish gray needles.

Cathaya argyrophylla. Extremely rare species from China. This photo, taken during his visit to Beijing (Peking), was made available by H. J. van de Laar.

Calocedrus decurrens 'Riet'. Grafted plant from the witches'-broom pictured in #56. Named after Mrs. van Hoey Smith. (1)

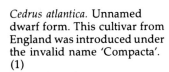

Cedrus atlantica. Unnamed dwarf form. This cultivar from England was introduced under the invalid name 'Compacta'. (1)

Cedrus atlantica 'Aurea'. The yellow-needled cultivar of the Atlas Cedar forms a small tree and retains a nice yellow in winter. (5)

Cedrus atlantica 'Fastigiata'. Columnar tree with grayish blue needles. Suitable for smaller gardens. (16)

Cedrus atlantica 'Glauca'. The universally grown blue Atlas Cedar. (46)

59

Cedrus atlantica 'Glauca'. The cones ripen only in the second year.

Cedrus atlantica 'Glauca Pendula'. Old tree in a French Arboretum. This weeping form should by no means be confused with 'Pendula', which 'weeps' a little less, but is much hardier. (42)

Cedrus atlantica 'Pendula'. This weeping form is fairly common in cultivation. The needles are greener than the preceding cultivar. (31)

Cedrus brevifolia. The short needles distinguish this species. Native only to the island of Cyprus where the remaining trees are strictly protected. (1)

Cedrus brevifolia. Cones. (1)

Cedrus deodara. The Himalayan Cedar. Unfortunately this fine tree often suffers in low winter temperatures. (7)

Cedrus deodara 'Albospica'. The silvery white twigs appear to full advantage, especially on young, vigorous trees.

Cedrus deodara 'Aurea'. The yellow-needled form of the Himalayan Cedar. This cultivar also dislikes severe winters. (15)

Cedrus deodara 'Gold Mound'. Novelty; may possibly enhance the present array of cultivars. (13)

Cedrus deodara 'Golden Horizon'. A new dwarf form originating in Boskoop, the Netherlands. Suitable for balconies and small gardens. The hardiness leaves something to be desired, just as in the other forms. (38)

Cedrus deodara 'Karl Fuchs'. This hardy form was selected from a seedling lot from Pakistanian seed. Not widely available. (62)

Cedrus deodara 'Lime Glow'. An Australian selection made by Don Teese. (38)

Cedrus deodara 'Pendula'. Weeping form. The habit of this cultivar varies depending on how the young plant was formed in the nursery. This low growing form is rarely seen. (29)

Cedrus deodara 'Pygmy'. A 15 year old plant. A fine dwarf form that deserves more attention. (38)

Cedrus deodara 'Robusta'. This cultivar has longer needles than usual.

63

Cedrus libani. Silhouette of the Cedar of Lebanon. This species usually lacks a continuous terminal stem and so is usually broader than high in cultivation. (44)

Cedrus libani 'Comte de Dijon'. Old plant of this dwarf form; can hardly be distinguished from *C. libani* 'Nana'. (1)

Cedrus libani 'Gold Tip'. Young plant found in Australia by Don Teese.

Cedrus libani 'Pendula'. Old tree in a Monte Carlo city park.

Cedrus libani 'Pendula'. Male inflorescences.

Cedrus libani 'Pendula'. Cones.

Cedrus libani 'Sargentii'. Well-known, practically creeping dwarf cultivar. Pictured here with *Juniperus sabina* 'Tamariscifolia'. (29)

Cephalotaxus fortunei. Old, heavily pruned bush. The needles are longer than those of the related *C. harringtonia*. (3)

Cephalotaxus fortunei. Male inflorescences.

Cephalotaxus fortunei. Fruit.

Cephalotaxus harringtonia. Low and spreading bush form. This species often becomes a much taller bush; hardier than *C. fortunei.* (59)

Cephalotaxus harringtonia. Male and female inflorescences.

Cephalotaxus harringtonia and *C. harr.* var. *drupacea.* Mature specimens. (21)

Cephalotaxus harringtonia 'Fastigiata'. A broad spreading branch develops at the base, that, if propagated by cutting, produces the cv. 'Prostrata'. (3)

Cephalotaxus harringtonia 'Fastigiata'. Young plant. Winter color. (28)

Chamaecyparis formosensis. This rare species can only be grown in mild climates. (28)

Chamaecyparis funebris. Sometimes classified under
Cupressus but because of the
small cones now classified
under *Chamaecyparis.* (19)

Chamaecyparis henryae. Sometimes classified under *C.
thyoides.* This species has only
been in cultivation since 1955.
(1)

Chamaecyparis lawsoniana
'Albovariegata'. Very old,
white variegated form. (15)

Chamaecyparis lawsoniana
'Alumigold'. Excellent sulfur-
yellow columnar form;
available since 1966. (15)

Chamaecyparis lawsoniana
'Alumii'. Widely grown bluish
gray, broad, columnar form.
Often planted as a hedge in
Belgium. (61)

Chamaecyparis lawsoniana
'Alumii Magnifica'. This form
remains somewhat narrower
than 'Alumii'. (61)

Chamaecyparis lawsoniana
'Argenteovariegata'. Detail of
the variegated twigs. Old form;
originating in Scotland.

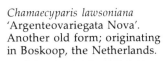

Chamaecyparis lawsoniana
'Argenteovariegata Nova'.
Another old form; originating
in Boskoop, the Netherlands.

Chamaecyparis lawsoniana
'Aurea', now *C.I.* 'Romana'.
Gigantic specimen in
southeast England. (37)

Chamaecyparis lawsoniana
'Aurea Romana'. A fairly new
selection. Very hardy. (18)

71

Chamaecyparis lawsoniana
'Aurea Densa'. Slow growing
dwarf form; originating in
England around 1930. (27)

Chamaecyparis lawsoniana 'Bleu
Nantais'. Nice blue cultivar;
originating in France. (21)

72   *Chamaecyparis lawsoniana* 'Blue
      Jacket'. Broad conical habit;
      introduced about 1932. (61)

Chamaecyparis lawsoniana 'Blue
Surprise'. Fairly slow growing,
bearing many juvenile
needles. Originated in the
Netherlands. (62)

Chamaecyparis lawsoniana
'Caudata'. Irregularly growing dwarf form introduced
about 1934 in Boskoop, the
Netherlands. (1)

Chamaecyparis lawsoniana
'Chilworth Silver'. Broadly
upright growing plants. Young
example. (61)

Chamaecyparis lawsoniana
'Columnaris'. This cultivar is
perhaps the best known of all
scale conifers. (38)

Chamaecyparis lawsoniana
'Darleyensis'. Fairly slow
growing, conical form;
introduced more than 100
years ago. (1)

Chamaecyparis lawsoniana 'Dart's Blue Ribbon'. One of the many upright, bluish gray cultivars. (61)

Chamaecyparis lawsoniana 'Dik's Weeping'. Peculiar, loose growing, weeping form. (17)

Chamaecyparis lawsoniana 'Drummondii'. Dark green, slow growing small tree. (61)

Chamaecyparis lawsoniana 'Elegantissima'. Close-up of a yellowish white, regular conical form; in use for mor than 100 years. (1)

Chamaecyparis lawsoniana 'Ellwoodii'. This common, conical form was discovered as a seedling in the Swanmore Park, England, about 1929. At the present time this cultivar is widely used as a small container plant. (23)

Chamaecyparis lawsoniana 'Ellwood's Pillar'. Also a mutation of 'Ellwoodii'; stays somewhat lower and narrower. The branching is even denser and thicker. (28)

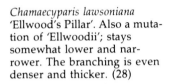

Chamaecyparis lawsoniana 'Ellwood's Gold'. Mutation of 'Ellwoodii'; the pale yellow twiglets lose but a little of their striking color in winter. (34)

Chamaecyparis lawsoniana 'Ellwood's White'. Developed from the grayish white branchlets that appear from time to time on 'Ellwoodii'. (38)

Chamaecyparis lawsoniana 'Erecta'. Columnar form with steeply upright branches. No longer available. This old tree dates back almost 100 years. (64)

Chamaecyparis lawsoniana 'Erecta Aurea'. Fairly low growing, conical form. Somewhat sensitive to frost, therefore often not attractive. (3)

Chamaecyparis lawsoniana 'Erecta Filiformis'. Young plant of a cultivar that has almost disappeared. Sometimes erroneously labeled 'Filiformis Compacta'. (2)

Chamaecyparis lawsoniana
'Erecta Viridis'. Commonly
cultivated fresh green,
columnar form; originating
from seeds collected in the
wild. (26)

Chamaecyparis lawsoniana
'Filifera'. Detail of the thread-
like twigs.

Chamaecyparis lawsoniana
'Filiformis Compacta'. This
dwarf form grows somewhat
slower and stays more compact
than the preceding. (7)

Chamaecyparis lawsoniana
'Filiformis'. Graceful, broad
conical habit with pendulous
twigs up to 3 m. Developed in
Belgium. (1)

77

Chamaecyparis lawsoniana
'Fletcheri'. Originated around
1911 as a mutation of the wild
species. This form looks
superficially like 'Ellwoodii'
but becomes much taller. (39)

Chamaecyparis lawsoniana
'Fletcher's Gold'. Differs from
'Fletcheri' in the soft yellow,
needlelike leaves. (1)

Chamaecyparis lawsoniana
'Fletcher's White'. Fairly fast
growing variegated mutation
of 'Fletcheri'. (28)

Chamaecyparis lawsoniana
'Forsteckensis'. Excellent,
widely grown dwarf form
for larger rock gardens. (61)

Chamaecyparis lawsoniana
'Fraseri'. Old cultivar, seldom
now in cultivation. Surpassed
by 'Columnaris' and similar
forms. (61)

Chamaecyparis lawsoniana
'Glauca Elegans'. Excellent,
fairly coarse scales, beautiful
silvery blue. (61)

Chamaecyparis lawsoniana
'Gimbornii'. Dwarf form
originating from seed in the
Von Gimborn Arboretum. (1)

Chamaecyparis lawsoniana
'Glauca Globus'. A form
selected about 1952 in Sopron,
Hungary. This cultivar has
unjustly been overlooked. (61)

Chamaecyparis lawsoniana
'Globosa'. Well-known, broad,
conical dwarf form. Developed
in the Netherlands. (3)

Chamaecyparis lawsoniana
'Globe'. Rare dwarf form;
developed in Hungary.
Seldom found in cultivation.
(7)

Chamaecyparis lawsoniana
'Golden King'. Yellow, conical,
small tree selected from
seedlings of *Chamaecyparis
lawsoniana* 'Triomf van
Boskoop'. (2)

Chamaecyparis lawsoniana
'Golden Triumph'. New form,
introduced in 1972; developed
in the Netherlands. (2)

Chamaecyparis lawsoniana
'Golden Wonder'. Cultivar
selected from seedlings;
introduced in 1963 and now
cultivated on a large scale. (61)

Chamaecyparis lawsoniana
'Grayswood Feather'. Slow
growing, thick, cigar-shaped
conifer. Appears to be a
valuable new cultivar. (75)

Chamaecyparis lawsoniana
'Grayswood Gold'. Same habit
as the preceding, but with
yellow foliage. (17)

Chamaecyparis lawsoniana
'Green Globe'. Small, globose
dwarf conifer with grayish
green needles. Not yet widely
available; appears to be
another excellent new cultivar,
especially for the rock garden.
(62)

Chamaecyparis lawsoniana
'Green Pillar'. This form looks
much like 'Erecta Viridis'.
Excellent for hedges. Developed in England shortly before
1940. (4)

Chamaecyparis lawsoniana
'Hillieri'. Nice yellow upright
cultivar with a somewhat loose
habit. (22)

Chamaecyparis lawsoniana
'Hollandia'. Nice, somewhat
open growing, upright tree.
The scale-like leaves are dark
emerald-green. (4)

Chamaecyparis lawsoniana
'Howarth's Gold'. Compact,
conical habit. Developed in
England. (61)

Chamaecyparis lawsoniana
'Imbricata Pendula'. Very
striking form with thread-like
twigs. Don Teese, Australia,
introduced this cultivar. (95)

Chamaecyparis lawsoniana
'Kilmacurragh'. Large spec-
imen in an Irish garden.
Introduced about 1950 by
Hillier. (21)

Chamaecyparis lawsoniana
'Kelleriis Gold'. Good, yellow,
columnar form; turns green in
the winter. (61)

Chamaecyparis lawsoniana
'Intertexta'. Originated in
Edinburgh more than 100
years ago. It is a handsome
tree with graceful, spreading
branches. (5)

Chamaecyparis lawsoniana
'Intertexta'. Close-up of the
scale-like leaves and cones.

Chamaecyparis lawsoniana
'Intertexta Pendula'. Broader
than the preceding form. Rare
in cultivation. The plant pictured is the original selection
beside which stands the emi-
nent dendrologist, the late Dr.
G. Krüssmann.

84

Chamaecyparis lawsoniana
'Konijn's Silver'. New white
variegated form. (4)

Chamaecyparis lawsoniana
'Kooy'. Bluish gray, columnar
form; developed in the 1920's,
but now scarce. (61)

...ana
...d yellow
...aps the
...llow
...(1)

Chamaecyparis lawsoniana
'Little Spire'. A cross between
'Fletcheri' and 'Wisselii'. (75)

Chamaecyparis lawsoniana
'Luna'. This cultivar was developed in Boskoop, the Netherlands. This silvery gray columnar has better form than 'Silver Queen', which it resembles. (102)

Chamaecyparis lawsoniana 'Lutea'. A greatly valued plant in England. Developed over 100 years ago. Somewhat sensitive to frost in cooler climates. (24)

Chamaecyparis lawsoniana 'Lutea Nana'. Broad, conical habit. Valuable but seldom planted. (1)

Chamaecyparis lawsoniana
'Lycopodioides'. Close-up of
a terminal branch. Selected
from seedlings approx. 100
years ago, but now rare. Not to
be confused with the cultivar of
the same name from *Cham.
pisifera.* (1)

Chamaecyparis lawsoniana
'Mass'. Introduced in the
Netherlands about 1957. It is a
slow growing, yellowish green
selection. (6)

Chamaecyparis lawsoniana
'Masonii'. Slow growing,
upright, conical form; very
hardy. (1)

Chamaecyparis lawsoniana
'Melfard'. Very hardy, but not
very attractive, columnar form.
(61)

87

Chamaecyparis lawsoniana 'Minima Aurea'. Well-known and very valuable; broad, conical cultivar. Closely resembles 'Aurea Densa', but has a somewhat looser habit. (1)

Chamaecyparis lawsoniana 'Minima'. Very old example of this rare dwarf form. (25)

Chamaecyparis lawsoniana 'Minima Glauca'. Plants sold under this name usually are 'Minima'. The true 'Minima Glauca' has grayish blue scales. It remains to be seen if the plant pictured here is correctly named. (1)

Chamaecyparis lawsoniana 'Moerheimii'. Tall, conical form with soft yellowish green foliage. (61)

Chamaecyparis lawsoniana 'Monumentalis Nova'. Columnar, somewhat open tree to 5–6 m. The twiglets are somewhat pendulous and grayish blue. (61)

Chamaecyparis lawsoniana 'Naberi'. Conical form with spreading branchlets. In the past it was also sold as yellow 'Triomf van Boskoop'. (61)

Chamaecyparis lawsoniana 'Nana'. A very old dwarf form. The 'Nana' forms always have a more or less continuous terminal branch. (1)

89

Chamaecyparis lawsoniana
'Nestoides'. Slow growing,
practically creeping cultivar;
developed in Canada. Re-
sembles the better known
'Tamariscifolia'. (40)

Chamaecyparis lawsoniana
'Nidiformis'. Originated in
Italy from seed. The original
plant, now 8 m broad, can be
found in Brissago, near Lake
Maggiore. (1)

Chamaecyparis lawsoniana
'Nova'. Loose growing, yellow,
globose form; developed in
Hungary. (7)

Chamaecyparis lawsoniana
'Nymans' is a fine, yellow
variegated form. Previously
labelled 'Nana Aureovariegata',
the correct name is now *C.l.*
'Handcross Park'. (1)

Chamaecyparis lawsoniana 'Olbrichii'. Conical, small tree originating in Switzerland. Seldom planted as there are better forms available. (2)

Chamaecyparis lawsoniana 'Parsons'. New, English cultivar. It is an interesting dwarf. Mrs. van Hoey Smith. (27)

Chamaecyparis lawsoniana 'Pembury Blue'. Beautiful, bluish gray, scale-like leaves. Fairly new selection. (61)

Chamaecyparis lawsoniana
'Pendula'. Markedly arching
pendulous branches distinguish this little known, small
tree. (62)

Chamaecyparis lawsoniana
'Pendula Vera'. Less markedly
pendulous than 'Pendula'. Has
long been in cultivation, but
remains relatively unknown.
Even if the plant is not staked a
good terminal develops. (1)

Chamaecyparis lawsoniana
'Pelt's Blue'. Fresh bluish gray,
conical form; newly developed
in Belgium. (17)

Chamaecyparis lawsoniana
'Pottenii'. Dark green, slender,
upright, columnar form. (103)

hamaecyparis lawsoniana
'ygmaea'. Applanated conical
rm, very slow growing, fresh
ark green. (75)

Chamaecyparis lawsoniana
'Pygmaea Argentea'. Old plant
in which the silvery gray color
is very pronounced. (24)

Chamaecyparis lawsoniana
'Rogersii'. Broad, conical dwarf
growing to 2 m tall. Cannot be
classified with the 'Nana'
group as it has a terminal. (7)

Chamaecyparis lawsoniana
'Robusta'Glauca'. Grows to
20 m tall. The scale-like leaves
are grayish blue. Not to
be confused with 'Glauca
Elegans', which it closely
resembles. (1)

Chamaecyparis lawsoniana
'Silver Queen.' Old, fairly tall
tree with silvery gray-green
foliage. Usually loose and
open; now surpassed by
'Luna'. (113)

Chamaecyparis lawsoniana
'Spek'. One of the best bluish
gray forms; introduced in 1942
in Boskoop, the Netherlands.
The habit is broadly conical,
the branching is somewhat
open. (61)

Chamaecyparis lawsoniana
'Stardust'. Fairly new cultivar
introduced in Boskoop, the
Netherlands. The habit is fairly
densely conical; color is sulfur-
yellow. (61)

Chamaecyparis lawsoniana
'Stewartii'. This is the best
known of all yellow upright
forms. Recently surpassed by
'Lane'. (2)

Chamaecyparis lawsoniana
'Stricta Aurea'. Slow growing,
broad, conical form; fairly rare.
(42)

Chamaecyparis lawsoniana
'Tamariscifolia'. Very large
specimen in an Irish garden.
Broad spreading, fairly fast
growing form that remains
low. (32)

Chamaecyparis lawsoniana
'Tharandtensis Caesia'. Young
plant. In this stage it can still be
considered a dwarf, but when
mature will outgrow this
classification.(61)

Chamaecyparis lawsoniana
'Tharandtensis Caesia'. This
semi-dwarf has been in cultivation for more than 100 years.
The late Sir Harold Hillier,
famous arborist and
dendrologist, is standing next
to this old specimen. (27)

95

Chamaecyparis lawsoniana 'Tilgate'. Applanated globose form developed in England. This form resembles 'Forsteckensis', but habit is more loose and open. (72)

Chamaecyparis lawsoniana 'Triomf van Boskoop'. This well-known cultivar has been on the market for almost a 100 years. It is still a highly commendable conifer. (103)

Chamaecyparis lawsoniana 'Versicolor'. Close-up of the young branches.

Chamaecyparis lawsoniana 'Westermannii'. A good yellow form with a somewhat loose habit. (61)

Chamaecyparis lawsoniana
'Winston Churchill'.
Handsome, yellow columnar
form; introduced in England
about 1945. (61)

Chamaecyparis lawsoniana
'Wisselii'. Narrow, conical
cultivar with the very characteristic twisted arrangement of
the leaves. (111)

Chamaecyparis lawsoniana
'Witzeliana'. Very small co-
lumnar form introduced by
Spaeth. (1)

Chamaecyparis lawsoniana
'Yellow Transparent'. This
conifer resembles a yellow
'Fletcheri'; introduced in
Boskoop, the Netherlands
in 1955. (61)

Chamaecyparis lawsoniana 'Youngii'. Old, dark green, conical cultivar. (21)

Chamaecyparis nootkatensis. Native to the western region of North America. Very hardy. (21)

Chamaecyparis nootkatensis 'Aureovariegata'. The young twigs are yellow variegated. (1)

Chamaecyparis nootkatensis 'Compacta'. Very old specimen in a Dutch pinetum. H. W. Vink, the late Dutch dendrologist, is seen standing next to it. (9)

Chamaecyparis nootkatensis
'Nidifera'. A dwarf developed
in Italy. The scale-like leaves
are bluish gray. (1)

Chamaecyparis nŏotkatensis
'Pendula'. Two types of this
well-known weeping tree are
in cultivation. Pictured here
the dense and full form with
pendulous branches. (103)

Chamaecyparis nootkatensis
'Pendula'. The branches of this
second form spread more
broadly and create a more
open habit. Seen here in the
garden of the Rabobank in
Boskoop, the Netherlands.

Chamaecyparis nootkatensis 'Variegata'. Twiglets are white variegated. (105)

Chamaecyparis obtusa. This species is native to Japan. Many garden forms have been derived this species. (1)

Chamaecyparis obtusa 'Aurea'. Close-up of a yellow-leaved form; now surpassed by 'Crippsii'. (42)

Chamaecyparis obtusa 'Chabo yadori'. Japanese cultivar with somewhat twisted twigs. (27)

Chamaecyparis obtusa 'Caespitosa'. A fine dwarf; very suitable for a small rock garden. (27)

Chamaecyparis obtusa 'Contorta'. Dwarf form, twiglets twisted; originated from seeds of 'Nana Gracilis'. (13)

Chamaecyparis obtusa 'Compacta'. Broad, low form; resembles the compact types of 'Nana Gracilis'. (1)

101

Chamaecyparis obtusa 'Coralliformis'. Dwarf form; resembles 'Lycopodioides' but remains much smaller. (61)

Chamaecyparis obtusa 'Crippsii'. Broad, conical habit, with superb fern-like foliage. Somewhat sensitive to frost in cooler climates. (61)

Chamaecyparis obtusa 'Draht'. Columnar habit; twigs resemble those of the well-known 'Lycopodioides'. (61)

Chamaecyparis obtusa
'Ericoides'. Juvenile form with
only juvenile leaves. Rare. (72)

Chamaecyparis obtusa
'Filicoides'. Often shrub-like,
with conspicuous feather-like
twigs. (1)

Chamaecyparis obtusa
'iliformis'. Detail of an old
lant. (41)

Chamaecyparis obtusa
'Flabelliformis'. Large plant in a
rock garden; this form grows
slowly. (29)

Chamaecyparis obtusa 'Fontana'. Resembles 'Crippsii' but has dark green foliage. (61)

Chamaecyparis obtusa 'Gimborn Beauty'. In the past, this form was also known as 'Gerda von Gimborn-Dietz'. (2)

Chamaecyparis obtusa 'Gimborn Beauty'. Detail of twigs.

Chamaecyparis obtusa
'Graciosa'. Mutation of 'Nana
Gracilis' originating in the
Netherlands about 1935. (1)

Chamaecyparis obtusa 'Gracilis'.
Japanese cultivar; somewhat
more compact and slower
growing than the species. (61)

Chamaecyparis obtusa
'Goldspire'. A new, upright
growing form. (13)

Chamaecyparis obtusa 'Hage'.
Broad, conical dwarf; discovered in the Netherlands in
1928. (1)

Chamaecyparis obtusa
'Juniperoides'. Dwarf form;
very slow growing at no more
than 1 cm per year. (23)

Chamaecyparis obtusa
'Juniperoides' and 'Nana
Aurea'. Good use of dwarf
conifers in a planter. (23)

Chamaecyparis obtusa 'Kosteri'.
This dwarf form grows very
slowly to hardly more than 1 m
high. (1)

Chamaecyparis obtusa 'Lutea Nova'. Very beautiful, up-right growing cultivar that is unfortunately somewhat sensitive to frost. (61)

Chamaecyparis obtusa 'Lycopodioides'. Close-up of young branches. The habit is often very irregular. (38)

Chamaecyparis obtusa 'Lycopodiodes Aurea'. Sulfur-yellow sport of the preceding cultivar. (61)

107

Chamaecyparis obtusa 'Mariesii'. This slow growing form has almost milk-white young twigs. Somewhat sensitive to direct sunlight. (1)

Chamaecyparis obtusa 'Minima'. Extremely slow growing; habit resembles 'Caespitosa'. (29)

Chamaecyparis obtusa 'Nana Lutea'. The scale-like leaves are vivid sulfur-yellow. (13)

Chamaecyparis obtusa 'Opaal'. Resembles the well-known 'Nana Gracilis', but the color of some branches is more yellowish green. (1)

Chamaecyparis obtusa 'Nana'.
Should by no means be
confused with the taller
growing 'Nana Gracilis'. (1)

Chamaecyparis obtusa 'Nana
Aurea'. Fairly slow growing;
resembles the widely grown
'Nana Gracilis' but has yellow
scales. (1)

Chamaecyparis obtusa 'Nana
Gracilis'. Beautiful dwarf
conifer; cultivated and planted
in large numbers worldwide.
(61)

109

Chamaecyparis obtusa 'Pygmaea'. Cultivated for a very long time. The color of this form is brownish green and in winter light brown. (38)

Chamaecyparis obtusa 'Repens'. Mutation of 'Nana Gracilis'; becomes much broader than high. (16)

Chamaecyparis obtusa 'Rigid Dwarf'. One of the most beautiful cultivars of *Chamaecyparis obtusa*. This form develops into a broad, conical plant of about 3 m. (1)

Chamaecyparis obtusa 'Tempelhof'. Fairly fast growing compact form. Developed in the Netherlands about 1964. (1)

Chamaecyparis obtusa
'Tetragona Aurea'. Detail of the
terminal branch of a young
tree.

Chamaecyparis obtusa
'Tetragona Aurea'. Even
though this form is styled as
a dwarf conifer it often grows
larger. (1)

Chamaecyparis obtusa 'Tonia'.
Very similar to 'Nana Gracilis'
but dotted with small, yellow-
white twiglets. (12)

Chamaecyparis obtusa
'Torulosa'. Detail of the
terminal branch of this peculiar
conifer. (1)

Chamaecyparis obtusa 'Verdun'.
A newer selection or mutation
from 'Nana Gracilis'. (61)

Chamaecyparis pisifera
'Argenteovariegata'. Detail of
the terminal branch of a
somewhat older plant.

Chamaecyparis obtusa 'Youngii'.
Widely grown in the past but
now scarce. Habit as the species, but the foliage is a soft
yellow. (2)

Chamaecyparis pisifera
'Boulevard'. Originated as
a mutation of 'Squarrosa'.
Widely grown. Very suitable
for flower boxes as a young
plant. (61)

Chamaecyparis pisifera 'Clouded Sky'. Also a mutation of 'Squarrosa'; fast growing. (2)

Chamaecyparis pisifera 'Clouded Sky'. Detail of a branch.

Chamaecyparis pisifera 'Golden Mop'. Mutation of 'Filifera Aurea'; somewhat more intense yellow and stays lower. (28)

Chamaecyparis pisifera 'Filifera'.
Small tree with threadlike
twigs. Definitely not a dwarf.
(1)

Chamaecyparis pisifera 'Filifera
Aureovariegata'. Remains low
growing; variegated with small
yellow spots. (63)

Chamaecyparis pisifera 'Filifera
Aurea'. Broad, conical semi-
dwarf form. The twigs are
threadlike and bright yellow.
(61)

Chamaecyparis pisifera 'Gold Spangle'. Also a mutation of 'Filifera Aurea'; grows faster and becomes much taller. (6)

Chamaecyparis pisifera 'Hime himuro'. Small dwarf of Japanese origin. (1)

Chamaecyparis pisifera 'Nana'. True dwarf form. Often confused with the faster growing 'Compacta'. (61)

Chamaecyparis pisifera
'Plumosa'. Tall tree with
feather-like foliage. There are
a number of related forms,
collectively called the
'Plumosa-group'. Note the
reddish brown trunk. (1)

Chamaecyparis pisifera
'Plumosa Albopicta'. Dwarf
form; dotted with white tipped
twigs. (3)

Chamaecyparis pisifera
'Plumosa Aurea Compacta'.
More compact, somewhat
aberrant, form of the preceding. (61)

Chamaecyparis pisifera
'Plumosa Aurea'. Well-known,
fast growing cultivar with
bronze-yellow foliage. (61)

Chamaecyparis pisifera
'Plumosa Flavescens'. Conical dwarf; the fine foliage is sulfur-yellow. (61)

Chamaecyparis pisifera
'Plumosa Compressa'. Densely branched, cushion-shaped shrub. (1)

Chamaecyparis pisifera
'Plumosa Juniperoides'. Looks very much like 'Plumosa Aurea Compacta' and is possibly identical to it. (1)

Chamaecyparis pisifera
'Plumosa Vera'. In the past this cultivar was commonly used as grafting understock. (2)

117

Chamaecyparis pisifera 'Pygmy'. Dense, globose form developed in England. (1)

Chamaecyparis pisifera 'Snow'. Dwarf form with almost white twiglets and scales. Beautiful plant. Quite susceptible to sunscald. (1)

Chamaecyparis pisifera 'Squarrosa Lombarts'. Stabile juvenile form; developed in the Netherlands. (6)

Chamaecyparis pisifera 'Squarrosa'. Very large specimen of a nearly forgotten cultivar. The frizzy foliage is sometimes used for greenery in flower arrangements. (76)

Chamaecyparis pisifera
'Squarrosa Sulphurea'. Sulfur-
yellow mutation of 'Squarrosa'.
(2)

Chamaecyparis pisifera
...ungold'. This new cultivar
...sembles 'Filifera Aurea', but
a duller yellow and hardier.
...1)

Chamaecyparis pisifera 'Tama-
himuro'. Developed in Japan
but little known in the West.
(1)

Chamaecyparis thyoides. Species native to the Eastern seaboard of the United States. Photographed in the Pine Barrens, of New Jersey.

Chamaecyparis thyoides 'Andelyensis'. Slow growing upright form; coloration is an attractive bluish green. (1)

Chamaecyparis thyoides 'Andelyensis Nana'. Looks much like the preceding but stays smaller and lower. (1)

Chamaecyparis thyoides 'Aurea'. Conical habit. In the winter bronze-yellow, in the summer bright yellow. (61)

hamaecyparis thyoides
'Compacta'. Old plant with
ontorted habit. (2)

Chamaecyparis thyoides
'Ericoides'. The winter color.
Fairly well-known dwarf form
with only juvenile needles.
(28)

Chamaecyparis thyoides
'Glauca'. Detail of twigs.

Chamaecyparis thyoides
'Glauca'. Graceful conical
form; more compact habit than
the species. (61)

121

Chamaecyparis thyoides
'Variegata'. Somewhat loose
and open growing; dotted with
yellow twiglets. (2)

Cryptomeria japonica.
Enormous old tree. (112)

Cryptomeria japonica. Young
and ripe cones on the same
tree.

122

ryptomeria japonica .raucarioides'. Old tree in urraghmore, Ireland. The edles are short and placed osely to the twigs. At times nfused with 'Gracilis'.

Cryptomeria japonica 'Bandai-sugi'. Well-known dwarf form; growth irregular, dull brownish green. (6)

Cryptomeria japonica 'Cristata'. Beautiful detail of a cockscomb. These are abundant on this cultivar.

Cryptomeria japonica 'Compacta'. Columnar tree, also called 'Lobbii Compacta'. (21)

Cryptomeria japonica
'Dacrydioides'. Shrub-like
habit. The needles are short
and stiff. (61)

Cryptomeria japonica 'Elegans'.
In the summer 'Elegans' is
fresh green, in the winter dark
brownish red. (5)

Cryptomeria japonica 'Globosa
Nana'. Very well-known dwarf
form for larger rock gardens.
(1)

Cryptomeria japonica 'Elegans
Aurea'. The needles are fresh
greenish yellow in the summer
but green in winter. (23)

ryptomeria japonica 'Gracilis'.
etail of needles, see also *C. j.*
raucarioides'.

Cryptomeria japonica 'Jindai-sugi'. Large specimen of this fairly slow growing form. (1)

ryptomeria japonica
ilmacurragh'. Detail of the
rminal; form developed in
eland. (58)

Cryptomeria japonica 'Knaptonensis'. Originated as a witches'-broom on 'Nana Albospica'. (40)

125

Cryptomeria japonica
'Littleworth Gnom'. American cultivar, rare in Europe. (75)

Cryptomeria japonica 'Lobbii'. Detail of terminal branch. This cultivar resembles 'Compacta', and is often confused with it. (1)

Cryptomeria japonica 'Monstrosa'. Old plant in Pancarron, Ireland.

Cryptomeria japonica 'Monstrosa Nana'. Excellent dwarf form; widely cultivated. (29)

126

Cryptomeria japonica 'Nana'. Very old dwarf form that was brought to England from China by Robert Fortune in 1846. (27)

Cryptomeria japonica 'Pygmaea'. Beautiful, small dwarf; unfortunately somewhat sensitive to frost. (13)

Cryptomeria japonica 'Rasensugi'. Detail of the peculiar twisted twigs. (1)

Cryptomeria japonica 'Rasensugi'. Fast growing, small tree; imported from Japan only about 20 years ago. (13)

Cryptomeria japonica 'Sekkan-sugi'. This slow growing plant has sulfur-yellow needles and branches; somewhat susceptible to sunscald. (1)

Cryptomeria japonica 'Spiralis'. Detail of the twisted branches. (1)

Cryptomeria japonica 'Spiraliter Falcata'. Dwarf form; probably originated as a mutation of 'Spiralis'. (128)

Cryptomeria japonica 'Variegata'. Very old form that was developed in Belgium. (1)

Cryptomeria japonica
'Vilmoriniana'. The well-
known French nursery,
Vilmorin, imported this dwarf
conifer from Japan as *Juniperus
japonica*. Curiously enough
'Vilmoriniana' is unknown in
Japan. (1)

Cryptomeria japonica 'Yoshino'.
loose growing cultivar; with
some pruning is very compact.
(8)

Cryptomeria japonica.
Cryptomeria is frequently used
for bonsai.

Cunninghamia lanceolata. Native to central China and quite hardy in temperate climates. (6)

Cunninghamia lanceolata 'Compacta'. Young plant, propagated by grafting. Probably originated from a witches'-broom. (1)

Cunninghamia lanceolata 'Glauca'. The needles are grayish blue. This tree is hardy in the temperate climates. (7)

Cunninghamia lanceolata. Cone and male inflorescences.

Cupressocyparis leylandii. Used both for hedges and as specimen trees. Planted in England as a wind screen. (21)

Cupressocyparis leylandii 'Castlewellan Gold'. In the summer a beautiful yellow, in the winter a bronze-yellow. (1)

Cupressocyparis leylandii 'Hyde Hall'. Light yellowish green conical dwarf form. (113)

131

Cupressocyparis leylandii 'Silver Dust'. An attractive white variegated form. (1)

Cupressocyparis notabilis. An older specimen of this rare hybrid. (43)

Cupressus arizonica. Large specimen of this fairly common species. Quite hardy in temperate climates. (21)

Cupressus arizonica. Typical color of the trunk is gray with brownish red spots.

Cupressus arizonica 'Aurea'. A form common in Tasmania. (94)

Cupressus arizonica 'Compacta'. Very slow growing dwarf form. (1)

Cupressus arizonica 'Crowborough'. Interesting Australian cultivar. (38)

133

Cupressus arizonica 'Fastigiata Aurea'. Fairly loose, conical form; developed in France. (45)

Cupressus arizonica 'Glauca'. This fairly hardy form is widely planted in temperate climates. (15)

Cupressus arizonica 'Sulfurea'. Grayish yellow, fairly slow growing conical conifer. Only moderately hardy in temperate regions. (1)

134

Cupressus arizonica 'Variegata'. The tips of the twigs are white variegated. (1)

Cupressus bakeri. A species native to northern California, U.S.A. The twigs smell of turpentine. (3)

Cupressus cashmeriana. Tropical species, native to India. Very suitable as an indoor plant. Large trees are growing in central France. (47)

Cupressus cashmeriana. Detail of twigs.

Cupressus guadalupensis. Rare cypress from Mexico. (73)

135

Cupressus lusitanica. A natural dwarf form in Portugal.

Cupressus macnabiana. Closely related to *C. bakeri.* Quite hardy in temperate regions. (1)

Cupressus macrocarpa 'Aurea'. Old tree in Canberra. Perhaps identical to 'Lutea'.

Cupressus macrocarpa 'Aurea'. Close-up view.

Cupressus macrocarpa 'Globe'. Applanated globose form. (38)

Cupressus macrocarpa 'Fastigiata'. Columnar form that sometimes appears in seedlings. (50)

137

Cupressus macrocarpa
'Greenstead Magnificent'.
Small plant that stays low.
Developed in Australia. (95)

Cupressus macrocarpa
'Goldcrest'. Distributed by an
English grower in Cornwall
about 1950, and now perhaps
the conifer of which the largest
number are propagated yearly.
'Goldcrest' is used as an indoor
plant. (1)

Cupressus macrocarpa
'Horizontalis Aurea'. A loose,
broad shrub. (113)

Cupressus macrocarpa 'Keown'.
Columnar form. Rare. (36)

Cupressus sempervirens 'Stricta'. The Italian Cypress; so-called because it is commonly planted in the vicinity of the Mediterranean.

Cupressus macrocarpa 'Lutea'. Very large specimen. The new foliage is an attractive yellow, but turns nearly green in the second year. (111)

Cupressus torulosa. This is a Chinese species; rarely planted in the West. (31)

Cupressus sempervirens 'Swane's Golden'. Cultivar from New Zealand. (96)

Dacrydium biforme. A nursery plant. Small tree from New Zealand where it grows in the mountain forests.

Dacrydium cupressinum. Also native to New Zealand. The juvenile form and the mature form pictured next to each other.

Dacrydium cupressinum and *Dicksonia* (Tree Fern). (96)

Dacrydium franklinii. Tree resembling a weeping cypress; native to Tasmania.

Dacrydium franklinii 'Pendulum'. A famous specimen in the garden on Garnish Island, Ireland.

Dacrydium kirkii. Native to New Zealand where it becomes a tree 25 m tall.

Dacrydium kirkii. Detail of the connated leaves.

141

Dacrydium laxifolium. Small creeping shrub; referred to as the smallest conifer in the world. Photographed in its native habitat, the mountains of New Zealand.

Dacrydium laxifolium. **Fruit.**

Diselma archeri. Very rare conifer from Tasmania. Seldom in cultivation elsewhere.

Diselma archeri. **Detail view.**

142

Fitzroya cupressoides. Detail of a branch with cones.

Fitzroya cupressoides. Very rare tree from southern Chile. Native to a small area in the Andes mountains. Can sometimes be found in arboreta in mild climates. (33)

Fokienia hodginsii. Detail of young foliage.

Fokienia hodginsii. This genus is also rare. Native to China. Hardy only in subtropical regions. (1)

143

Glyptostrobus lineatus.
Deciduous Chinese conifer;
probably extinct in the wild.
Very rare. Hardy only in
subtropical areas. (36)

Juniperus bermudiana. A nursery
plant in New Zealand. This
species is native only to the
Bermuda Islands.

Juniperus cedrus. Detail of
branches. Native to the Canary
Islands but practically extinct.

Juniperus chinensis. Very common tree in China. This species is frequently used as a rootstock for garden forms. (1)

Juniperus chinensis. Widely used for bonsai.

Juniperus chinensis. 'Aurea'. Slow growing, attractive, yellow form. (6)

Juniperus chinensis 'Blue Alps'. Somewhat pendulous form; recently introduced. (28)

Juniperus chinensis 'Blue Point'.
Dense, compact, conical form;
mildly susceptible to mildew.
(17)

Juniperus chinensis
'Echiniformis'. Hedgehog-
shaped globe; in a rock garden.
(77)

Juniperus chinensis 'Fairview'.
American cultivar selected
from seedlings; narrow,
conical habit. (61)

146

Juniperus chinensis 'Japonica'. An odd name. Some branches bear needles while others bear scale-like leaves. (6)

Juniperus chinensis 'Kaizuka Variegated'. Similar to the preceding but dotted with yellow variegated twiglets. (34)

Juniperus chinensis 'Kaizuka'. Graceful, shrub-like; fairly broad and tall growing. (1)

147

Juniperus chinensis 'Keteleeri'. Commonly cultivated, beautiful tree form; always bears rich blue, cone berries. (85)

Juniperus chinensis 'Maney'. Shrub-like semi-dwarf conifer. Developed in the U.S.A. about 1935. (4)

Juniperus chinensis 'Monarch'. Narrow, conical tree. This beautiful cultivar drops its dead needles, so it always looks attractive. (104)

Juniperus chinensis 'Neaboriensis'. It is possible that this form was collected in China by Father David and brought to Europe. (1)

Juniperus chinensis 'Obelisk'. An American selection. (1)

Juniperus chinensis 'Robusta Green'. Beautiful, upright form; as yet relatively rare. (17)

Juniperus chinensis 'Olympia'. Slender, columnar form; selected from Japanese seed. (61)

149

Juniperus chinensis
'Sheppardii'. Shrub. Brought
from China by Fortune. (1)

Juniperus chinensis 'Stricta'.
Widely cultivated in the past
though less frequently cultivated today because it is susceptible to mildew. (4)

Juniperus chinensis 'Stricta
variegata'. Similar to the
preceding but dotted with
white twiglets. (2)

Juniperus chinensis 'Templar'.
Novelty, but with a future. (20)

Juniperus communis. Three different growth habits displayed in the National Park, 'De Hoge Veluwe', the Netherlands.

Juniperus communis. Cone berries.

Juniperus chinensis 'Variegata'.
Detail of a variegated branch.

Juniperus communis
'Compressa'. Very tight columnar form. Slow growing.
(115)

Juniperus communis 'Cracovica'.
This cultivar was discovered
125 years ago near Kraków,
Poland. (4)

Juniperus communis, 'Depressa Aurea'. Beautiful, low growing cultivar. (52)

Juniperus communis 'Echiniformis'. Small hedge-hog-shaped conifer; very suitable for a small rock garden. (29)

Juniperus communis 'Effusa'. A form that stays low and looks much like 'Repanda'. (1)

Juniperus communis 'Fontaen'. Attractive novelty from Germany. Leaves feel sharp. (6)

Juniperus communis 'Gold Cone'. Yellow-needled form of the columnar type. (4)

Juniperus communis 'Hornibrookii'. Very well-known low growing form. Leaves feel sharp, in contra to 'Repanda'. (105)

Juniperus communis 'Horstmann'. Beautiful, weeping form; still rare. (63)

Juniperus communis ssp. nar Photographed near Ulriker Switzerland. The mountain form of the common Junip Berry.

154

Juniperus communis 'Nana
urea'. Practically creeping
rm with golden yellow
edles. (17)

Juniperus communis 'Oblonga
Pendula'. Older plants in a
French nursery. (45)

Juniperus communis 'Repanda'.
'idely planted cultivar; re-
ains low. Winter color a
ded brownish green. The
edles are not sharp. (4)

Juniperus communis var.
saxatilis. Also known as var.
montana. Growing in the wild
on Hurricane Ridge in North
America.

155

Juniperus communis 'Sentinel'.
This small columnar form is
also called 'Little Soldier'. (6)

Juniperus communis 'Suecica'.
Very commonly cultivated
plant; several selections are
available.

Juniperus conferta. This species
is native to the beaches of
northern Japan and Sachalin.
Only moderately hardy. (113)

Juniperus communis 'Velebit'. A
dwarf form with fairly long
needles. Discovered in Yugoslavia. (13)

Juniperus conferta 'Blue Pacific'.
Differs from the species in the
much bluer needles. (20)

Juniperus davurica 'Expansa'.
In the past this well-known
cultivar was classified under *J.
chinensis*. (7)

Juniperus davurica 'Expansa
Variegata'. White twiglets are
scattered over the plant. (7)

157

Juniperus deppeana. North American species. One of the bluest of the *Juniperus* species. (12)

Juniperus deppeana. The plant pictured here is labeled *J. pachyphlaea;* these two names are synonymous. (7)

Juniperus horizontalis. The native habitat is very extensive, almost all of North America. Plants labeled as *J. horizontalis* are usually the cv. 'Prostrata'. (1)

Juniperus drupacea. The long needles distinguish this south European species from its closest relative, *J. communis.* (113)

Juniperus horizontalis 'Alpina'. Note peculiar deviant habit of upright branches. (16)

Juniperus horizontalis 'Andorra Compact'. An American selection from the old 'Plumosa'. In the winter this form turns a peculiar lilac-brown. (106)

Juniperus horizontalis 'Bar Harbor'. Good mat forming plant growing over a wall. (28)

Juniperus horizontalis 'Blue Acres'. One of the many new American introductions. (17)

Juniperus horizontalis 'Grey Pearl'. New form; not suitable as a ground cover due to its upright habit. (6)

Juniperus horizontalis 'Plumosa' in summer. (15)

Juniperus horizontalis 'Douglasii'. Without doubt this is the bluest cultivar of all. However, it does not easily form a dense mat. (7)

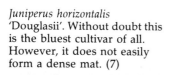

Juniperus horizontalis 'Emerald Spreader'. Excellent new American cultivar; grayish green color. (16)

niperus horizontalis 'Blue
hip'. (6)

Juniperus horizontalis 'Hughes'.
Very valuable ground cover.
(15)

niperus horizontalis 'Jade
iver'. One of the newest
rms; a beautiful grayish
een silvery color. (14)

Juniperus horizontalis
'Marcellus'. A mat forming
plant. Still rare. (1)

Juniperus horizontalis 'Plumosa'.
The winter color. An old, taller
form, now surpassed by
'Andorra Compact'. (5)

Juniperus horizontalis 'Prince of
Wales'. Discovered in Canada
in Banff National Park. (14)

Juniperus horizontalis
'Prostrata'. Excellent green;
mat forming plant. (7)

Juniperus horizontalis 'Wiltonii'.
Often found labeled 'Glauca',
which is incorrect and should
be discontinued. (2)

niperus horizontalis 'Winter
ue'. A distinctive winter
lor distinguishes this muta-
on of 'Plumosa'. (28)

Juniperus × *media* 'Blaauw'.
Imported from Japan about
1924. Belongs to the 'Plumosa
group'. (32)

Juniperus × *media* 'Blue
and Gold'. Mutation of
'Pfitzeriana'. (15)

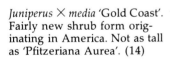

Juniperus × *media* 'Gold Coast'.
Fairly new shrub form originating in America. Not as tall
as 'Pfitzeriana Aurea'. (14)

163

Juniperus × *media* 'Golden Saucer'. Mutation of 'Pfitzeriana Aurea'; more compact habit. (15)

Juniperus × *media* 'Hetzii'. Large shrub, sometimes growing into a small tree. (16)

Juniperus × *media* 'Mint Julep'. An American cultivar. Markedly influenced by *J. sabina*. (2)

Juniperus × *media* 'Mordigan Gold'. Another mutation of 'Pfitzeriana Aurea'. (20)

Juniperus × media 'Old Gold'. A mutation of 'Pfitzeriana Aurea' originating in Boskoop. Remains much lower and has a fine yellow winter color. (12)

Juniperus × media 'Pfitzeriana'. Widely planted large shrub form. Probably brought from north China by Father David. (5)

Juniperus × media 'Pfitzeriana compacta'. A more compact growing mutation. (1)

Juniperus × media 'Pfitzeriana Aurea'. The same habit as the preceding but with yellow twigs and needles. (5)

Juniperus × *media* 'Pfitzeriana
Glauca'. Somewhat loose
habit. Fine silvery blue foliage.
Quite difficult to transplant. (1)

Juniperus × *media* 'Plumosa
Aurea'. Well-known, beautiful
cultivar. (1)

Juniperus × *media* 'Plumosa
Aureovariegata'. The same
habit as the preceding. Green
foliage is dotted with yellow
twiglets. (114)

Juniperus × media 'Sulphur Spray'. A sulfur-yellow sport from 'Hetzii'. (86)

Juniperus occidentalis. Native to western North America.

Juniperus osteosperma. Native to western North America; photographed on the Tioga Pass. Usually shrub-like.

Juniperus oxycedrus.
Spontaneous dwarf form; in
the wild near Pec, Yugoslavia.

Juniperus oxycedrus. Cone
berries. Native to the
Mediterranean region.

Juniperus phoenicia.
Mediterranean species;
growing near Ifrane, North
Africa.

Juniperus phoenicia. Cone
berries.

Juniperus procumbens 'Bonin Islands'. Beautiful creeping form, better known as 'Nana', but remains smaller and more compact. (62)

Juniperus procumbens 'Nana'. Beautiful specimen planted in a hole in a wall. (54)

Juniperus recurva. Native to the Himalayas. Barely hardy in temperate climates. (118)

169

Juniperus recurva 'Viridis'. A greener form. (28)

Juniperus recurva 'Castlewellan'. Old cultivar; differing from the species in that the branches weep more. (36)

Juniperus rigida. Native to Korea and Manchuria. Very hardy, yet rarely planted. (2)

Juniperus sabina 'Buffalo'. Originated from Russian seeds. (6)

Juniperus sabina. In cultivation since antiquity; native to all of central and southern Europe. (28)

Juniperus sabina 'Calgary Carpet'. New form from Canada. Note the feather-like twigs. (14)

Juniperus sabina 'Fastigiata'. Somewhat irregular columnar form. Young plants often do not display their final habit. (2)

Juniperus sabina 'Rockery Gem'. Also classified under *J. chinensis* or *J. × media*. Developed in Boskoop, the Netherlands. (6)

Juniperus sabina 'Tamariscifolia'. Widely planted low growing form. Unfortunately, susceptible to twig blight and mildew. (1)

Juniperus sabina 'Variegata'. A white variegated form. (15)

Juniperus sargentii 'Glauca'. Slow growing. The forms included in *J. sargentii* are also classified under *J. chinensis*. (7)

Juniperus scopulorum 'Glauca Pendula'. The name of the weeping tree shown here is possibly not valid. It is a very rare form. (63)

Juniperus scopulorum 'Moonlight'. Most cultivars belonging to *J. scopulorum* are difficult to grow in light soils. They often suffer from twig blight. (17)

Juniperus scopulorum 'O'Connor'. Broad, upright, shrub form. (6)

173

Juniperus scopulorum 'Sierra Silver'. Detail of the terminal branch of a young plant. (1)

Juniperus scopulorum 'Wichita Blue'. An upright form with silvery blue foliage. (20)

Juniperus scopulorum 'Springbank'. One of the few cultivars that grows well in light soil.

Juniperus squamata 'Blue Carpet'. Excellent, new flat growing cultivar developed in the Netherlands. (28)

174

Juniperus silicicola. Native to North America.

Juniperus silicicola. Close-up of trunk.

Juniperus squamata 'Blue Spider'. Looks a little like 'Blue Carpet', but the center of the plant is quite a bit higher. (108)

Juniperus squamata 'Blue Star'. A Dutch cultivar originating from a witches'-broom on 'Meyeri'. (4)

Juniperus squamata
'Campbellii'. Small, columnar
form; rare. (29)

Juniperus squamata 'Chinese
Silver'. Small, weeping tree;
only rarely cultivated. (114)

Juniperus squamata 'Glassell'.
Applanated globose form. (1)

Juniperus squamata var. *fargesii*.
Native to the border region
of Tibet, Nepal and India. A
broad, conical plant. (36)

Juniperus squamata 'Holger'. Some confusion exists with this cultivar in name/description. The typical 'Holger' is sulfur-yellow in the summer. (1)

Juniperus squamata 'Hunnetorp'. This "sister plant" of 'Holger' is often confused with it. (28)

Juniperus squamata 'Loderi'. Shrub-like. Developed in England by Sir Edmund Loder. Rare. (61)

177

Juniperus squamata 'Meyeri'.
Widely cultivated, well-known
shrub form. The dead needles
are retained and give older
plants a somewhat untidy
appearance. (1)

Juniperus squamata 'Meyeri'.
Variegated twiglets. A sport;
not yet named. (15)

Juniperus squamata 'Pygmaea'.
Compact shrub that does not
creep. (29)

Juniperus squamata var. *sinensis*. Thick, conical plant. Very rare. (29)

Juniperus squamata 'Wilsonii'. Collected in China in 1909 by Wilson and sent to the United States. (1)

Juniperus virginiana 'Blue Cloud'. Shrub form derived from a cross with *J. chinensis*. (7)

Juniperus virginiana. Photographed in the Tennessee Valley, U.S.A. Excellent timber tree.

Juniperus virginiana. A narrow, columnar form and the typical trunk. (78)

Juniperus virginiana 'Burkii'. Widely grown in the 1950's. (28)

180

Juniperus virginiana 'Fiore'.
Novelty from the U.S.A. (17)

Juniperus virginiana 'Canaertii'.
...road, columnar form with
...esh, dark green foliage. Very
...ardy. (15)

...niperus virginiana 'Frosty
...lorning'. Irregular shrub form
...ith silvery blue foliage. Still
...re. (16)

Juniperus virginiana 'Glauca'.
Common, upright conifer with
beautiful bluish gray foliage.
(110)

Juniperus virginiana 'Globosa'. Globose form rarely found in nurseries. (1)

Juniperus virginiana 'Greenspire'. Narrow, columnar form of unknown origin. (17)

Juniperus virginiana 'Grey Owl'. Beautiful shrub form with silvery blue foliage. Originated in a Dutch nursery from a chance cross with *J. media* 'Pfitzeriana'. (28)

Juniperus virginiana 'Hillii'. Once quite common but now scarce. (2)

182

niperus virginiana 'Lemon
ll'. Small, shrub form; slow
owing. (6)

Juniperus virginiana
'Moonglow'. Looks like
'Skyrocket' but is much
broader. Also classified
under *J. scopulorum*. (13)

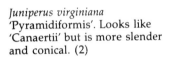

Juniperus virginiana
'Pyramidiformis'. Looks like
'Canaertii' but is more slender
and conical. (2)

Juniperus virginiana 'Pendula'.
Irregular, somewhat untidy,
weeping tree. (1)

183

Juniperus virginiana 'Spartan'.
Excellent new columnar form;
fresh dark green. Young plants
grow irregularly. Also known
as 'Helle'. (17)

Juniperus virginiana 'Skyrocket'.
Popular conifer in the heather
garden, where it quickly becomes too large. Pictured with
Cedrus atlantica 'Pendula'. (87)

Juniperus virginiana 'Tripartita'.
Widely grown in the past, but
now surpassed by the many
superior forms of *J.* × *media*. (3)

184

Keteleeria davidiana. A tree resembling *Abies;* however, the cones differ markedly. Native to China.

Larix decidua. Cones.

Larix decidua. European *Larix* or Larch. (35)

Keteleeria fortunei. A large tree
in an Australian botanical
garden. Native to China.

Keteleeria fortunei. A branch
with young and mature cones.

Larix decidua 'Compacta'. Extremely small plant in autumn
color. Reminiscent of topiary
figures created with *Taxus* or
Buxus. (55)

186

Larix decidua 'Corley'. Witches'-
broom. (28)

Larix decidua 'Pendula'. A tall, slender, upright tree of a weeping form. (131)

Larix gmelinii var. *japonica*. Native to northern Japan and Manchuria. (56)

Larix gmelinii var. *japonica*. New foliage in early spring.

Larix kaempferi. The Japanese *Larix* is at least as common as the European *Larix*. (5)

187

Larix griffithiana. Native to the Himalaya mountains. (119)

Larix griffithiana. Cones.

Larix kaempferi 'Blue Rabbit'. One of the few Larches with bluish green needles. (42)

Larix kaempferi 'Georgengarten'. Witches'-broom. (64)

rix kaempferi 'Pendula'. Old
ample of the Japanese
eping *Larix*. (65)

Larix kaempferi 'Prostrata'.
A creeping form. If staked it
can be formed into a small,
weeping tree. (1)

rix laricina. American Larch.
owering.

Libocedrus bidwillii. Trunk with
young foliage. Subtropical
species. (120)

189

Metasequoia glyptostroboides.
Cones develop on fairly young
trees.

Microbiota decussata. Summer
color. An east Siberian species;
only available in the last fif-
teen years. Introduced by
Arboretum Trompenburg, the
Netherlands. (1)

Microbiota decussata. In the
winter *Microbiota* colors a
brownish gray. (1)

Microbiota decussata. Cones
with seeds. First discovered in
the Arboretum Trompenburg,
the Netherlands. (1)

Microcachrys tetragona. In the wild near Lake Dobson, Tasmania.

Microcachrys tetragona. Detail of the leaves and the male inflorescence.

Microstrobus fitzgeraldii. Native to Tasmania. (38).

Microstrobos niphophilus. In the
wild near Lake Dobson,
Tasmania.

Microstrobos niphophilus. Male
inflorescence.

Neocallitropsis araucarioides.
Herbarium material in the Kew
Gardens, U.K. This is an ex-
tremely rare conifer.

Papuacedrus arfakensis.
Extremely rare; tropical conifer
native to New Guinea. (22)

Phyllocladus alpinus. In Otari,
New Zealand, Native Plant
Museum. The species of this
genus do not look at all like
conifers but leaves are con-
structed like the needles of
conifers. Native to New
Zealand.

Phyllocladus alpinus. Detail of
the leaves and the seeds.

Phyllocladus asplenifolius. Detail
of the leaves and the inflorescences.

Phyllocladus asplenifolius.
Photographed growing in the
wild. This species is native to
Tasmania.

193

Phyllocladus glaucus. Leaves and male and female inflorescences. This species also comes from New Zealand.

Phyllocladus trichomanoides. Leaves.

Picea abies. Spontaneous dwarf form in the mountains near Derborance, Switzerland.

Picea abies 'Acrocona'. This cultivar bears cones at the ends of young shoots. A widely planted cultivar; discovered in the wild in Sweden. (5)

Picea abies. The common spruce distributed over all of Europe. Growing near Klosters in east Switzerland.

Picea abies. The seeds of the common spruce are a favorite food of squirrels.

Picea abies. Grayish white trunks. Pictured in a Swiss production forest.

195

Picea abies 'Aurea Magnifica'. This spruce is especially bright yellow in the winter. (62)

Picea abies 'Capitata'. Old cultivar; irregular growing, semi-dwarf. (4)

Picea abies 'Clanbrassiliana'. Short-needled dwarf form which grows very slowly. The original plant is still alive in the Tollymore Gardens in Ireland. (1)

Picea abies 'Compacta'. Compact and truly globose plant with very short needles. (12)

Picea abies 'Cranstonii'. Also called 'Snake Spruce'. (65)

Picea abies 'Cupressina'. Slender, columnar form; better than 'Pyramidata', which grows much broader. (105)

ea abies 'Diffusa'. Dense bose form; rather rare. (27)

Picea abies 'Emsland'. Fresh green columnar form; recommendable. (61)

197

Picea abies 'Farnsburg'.
Selected in Switzerland from
seeds of 'Inversa'. This cultivar
grows slowly and forms a
miniature, weeping tree. (12)

Picea abies 'Formanek'. A new
cultivar from Pruhonice,
Czechoslovakia. (1)

Picea abies 'Frohburg'. Excellent
weeping spruce of Swiss
origin. (61)

Picea abies 'Hillside Upright'.
American columnar form. Rare
elsewhere. (71)

Picea abies 'Gregoryana
Veitchii'. More compact habit
and shorter needles than the
preceding. (61)

...ea abies 'Gregoryana'.
...planated globose form; has
...endency to form ever faster-
...owing new shoots. (28)

...cea abies 'Hystrix'. Beautiful,
...ow growing, dwarf form. (12)

Picea abies 'Inversa'. Widely
grown weeping spruce. Often
planted in cemeteries. (3)

Picea abies 'Little Gem.' Originated as a witches'-broom from 'Nidiformis'. Very slow growing; discovered in the Netherlands. (4)

Picea abies 'Nidiformis'. Widely planted dwarf spruce. Remains low. (61)

Picea abies 'Obergaertner Bruns'. A beautiful plant with an impossible name. (20)

Picea abies 'Ohlendorffii'. One of the standard spruce cultivars. Old plants are often difficult to identify. (61)

Picea abies 'Pachyphylla'. A peculiar plant; unfortunately it is also very difficult to propagate. (27)

ea abies 'Phylicoides'. houette of an old tree. The edles are very short. (36)

Picea abies 'Pendula Major'. Selection from *P. abies* f. *pendula;* found in the wild. (12)

Picea abies 'Procumbens'. Broad growing shrub, much broader than high. Closely related to 'Repens'. (2)

Picea abies 'Pumila Nigra'. An old plant. Widely cultivated dwarf form. (3)

Picea abies 'Pyramidata'. Broad conical form. 'Cupressina' is nicer. (62)

Picea abies 'Pygmaea'. A globose form. Several different forms are on the market under this name; there are also more conical types. (1)

Picea abies 'Reflexa'. This cultivar is nothing more than a staked-up 'Inversa'. (27)

Picea abies 'Remontii'. One of the finest conical dwarf spruce. (61)

Picea abies 'Repens'. Old specimen. Growth is much broader than high. (3)

203

Picea abies 'Rubra Spicata'. Very
peculiar form; seldom planted.
(34)

Picea abies 'Tabuliformis'. Discovered as a witches'-broom in
the Trianon in Paris, France.
(27)

Picea abies 'Viminalis'. Photographed near Saas, Switzerland. This deviant form is occasionally found in the wild.

Picea abies 'Wartburg'. A broad
growing, weeping tree; developed in Switzerland. (2)

Picea abies 'Virgata'. Silhouette of the terminal branch. Needles resemble those of 'Cranstonii'.(2)

Picea abies 'Virgata'. Cones.

Picea abies 'Will's Zwerg'. Beautiful semi-dwarf conifer. Scarce. (61)

Picea alcoquiana. Cones. Better known as *P. bicolor* in the past.

205

Picea alcoquiana 'Howell's Tigertail'. Broad growing branches ascend at the ends; an American selection. (62)

Picea alcoquiana 'Prostrata'. Completely prostrate. (1)

Picea asperata. Fairly rare in cultivation. Related to *P. pungens*. (28)

Picea brachytyla. A rare spruce; short-needled and densely branched. (5)

Picea breweriana. Photographed in the Siskiyou Range, southern Oregon, U.S.A. A rare species.

Picea breweriana. Fine specimen. This species is often more attractive in cultivation than in the wild. (39)

Picea breweriana. Male inflorescences.

Picea engelmannii 'Glauca'.
Good, upright spruce with
grayish blue needles. (61)

Picea engelmannii. An unnamed
dwarf form. (62)

Picea glauca. Cones. Native to
Canada where it forms large
forests.

Picea engelmannii 'Snake'.
Bizarre form. (1)

Picea glauca var. *albertiana*. The wild variety; native to the province of Alberta, Canada. (61)

...cea glauca 'Alberta Globe'. ...utation of the well-known *...onica*'; globose. (62)

Picea glauca 'Aurea'. Yellow-needled form. (62)

Picea glauca 'Caerulea'. The needles, especially on the underside, are silvery blue. (61)

Picea glauca 'Conica'. Commonly grown dwarf. Often used as a Christmas tree. Excellent for containers on patios and balconies. (1)

Picea glauca 'Echiniformis'. Originated from a witches'-broom. Commonly cultivated valuable dwarf spruce. (62)

Picea glauca 'Laurin'. Mutation of 'Conica' but much denser and smaller. (1)

Picea glauca 'Lilliput'. Dwarf form developed in North America. Rare. (12)

Picea × *hurstii*. This is a hybrid of *P. pungens* and *P. engelmannii*; introduced in 1938. (61)

Picea jezoensis. Japanese Spruce. The top of the tree with cones. The underside of the needles is conspicuously silvery grayish white.

Picea jezoensis var. *hondoensis*. The top of a young tree with cones. A geographical variety of the preceding species. (6)

211

Picea jezoensis. A yet unnamed flat-growing dwarf. Now and then offered as 'Nana', however this name is invalid. (62)

Picea jezoensis 'Yosawa'. From a witches'-broom. (63)

Picea koyamai. A rare Japanese species found only on the island of Honshu; only several hundred trees are left. Related to *P. abies.* (2)

Picea likiangensis var. *balfouriana.* The needles are grayish-blue; habit is regularly conical. (13)

...cea likiangensis. Male and ...male inflorescences. Native ...central China. This species is ...ry hardy, but is rarely ...anted in the West.

Picea likiangensis. Cones.

...rea likiangensis var. *purpurea.* ...e buds of this variety are ...ncealed by the adjacent ...edles. The dark green color ...in contrast to the preceding ...riety. (13)

Picea mariana 'Argenteo-variegata'. The needles are almost completely white and often burn in direct sunlight.

Picea mariana. Large tree; forms forests from Labrador to Alaska. (69)

Picea mariana. The top of the tree with many, small cones.

Picea mariana 'Dumettii'. Widely cultivated in the past but now quite rare. (28)

Picea mariana 'Nana'. Old plant of this fine cultivar. There is probably more than one form in cultivation. (28)

Picea × *mariorika* 'Machala'.
Very nice, low growing spruce
originating in Czechoslovakia.
A hybrid between *P. mariana*
and *P. omorika.* (61)

Picea meyeri. Female inflorescences.

Picea morrisonicola. Native to
Taiwan and very hardy. (3)

Picea obovata. The natural distribution stretches from Siberia to the east coast of the Pacific Ocean. Related to *Picea abies.* Very hardy. (62)

Picea omorika. Male inflorescences.

Picea omorika. The terminal branch of a young tree, densely set with small dark purple cones. (61)

cea omorika 'Expansa'.
actically recumbent habit. If
e grafts from this form, the
fspring do not retain this
bit but grow upright. (1)

cea omorika 'Gnom'. This
all globose form is also
ssified under *P.* × *mariorika*.
)

Picea omorika 'Nana'. Witches'-
broom originally discovered in
Boskoop, the Netherlands.
Many plants of this form have
been grafted and distributed.
The habit is often irregular.
Occasionally a slow growing,
terminal branch is formed. (28)

217

Picea omorika 'Pendula'.
Weeping tree that stays small.
The branches hang almost
straight down. (61)

Picea omorika 'Pendula Bruns'.
A German selection that is
even more pendulous than the
preceding. (61)

Picea omorika 'Pimoko'. Low
growing dwarf; from a
witches'-broom. (63)

Picea orientalis. The Caucasian
Spruce. Photographed near
Trebizond (Turkey) at 1900 m
elevation. The needles are
much shorter than in other
Picea species.

218

Picea orientalis 'Aurea'. Old specimen. The young foliage is a nice golden yellow that later becomes dark green. Maaike van Hoey Smith keeps a watchful eye on it all. (1)

Picea orientalis. Young tree. In cultivation they usually grow somewhat broader than those found in nature. (2)

Picea orientalis 'Aurea Compacta'. Young plant of this semi-dwarf. (62)

219

Picea orientalia 'Early Gold'.
Mutation of 'Aurea'; originating in the Netherlands. (62)

Picea orientalis 'Skylands'. A
new, beautiful yellow, slender,
small tree. The needles of this
cultivar remain yellow in winter. (1)

Picea polita. Cones. Also known
as *P. torano.* The thick needles
are arranged radially and are
unpleasantly sharp.

Picea pungens 'Aurea'. The top
of a fairly young tree. The
needles are sulfur-yellow and
seldom burn in the sun. (99)

cea pungens 'Blue Trinket'.
are dwarf form colored a
mewhat dull-gray. The plant
comes fairly tall. (14)

Picea pungens 'Endtz'. One of
the many selections of the
well-known Blue Spruce. In
the past every nursery had
its own type; 'Endtz' has now
practically disappeared. (61)

cea pungens 'Fat Albert'. This
lection appears to have a
and future. In the U.S.A. it is
nsidered to be the best Blue
ruce. This cultivar does not
ed to be staked because it
rms an excellent terminal.
actically unknown in
rope. (13)

Picea pungens f. *glauca*. Cones of
a Blue Spruce seedling.

221

Picea pungens 'Glauca Globosa'. Also known as 'Globosa'. One of the few forms of *P. pungens* that can be propagated from cuttings. Commonly known and excellent for the small garden. (13)

Picea pungens 'Glauca Pendula Somewhat older plant. The habit is often very irregular. (1

Picea pungens 'Glauca Pro-cumbens'. Practically recum-bent shrub; photographed between the *Erica carnea* 'Winter Beauty'. (1)

Picea pungens 'Hoopsii'. This is
~~rhaps~~ the bluest of all, but is
~~ficult~~ to propagate and also
~~fficult~~ to form into a good
~~ee~~. (61)

Picea pungens 'Hoto'. Developed in Boskoop, the Netherlands. Selected because it
grows well and is fairly easy to
propagate. (104)

Picea pungens 'Iseli Fastigiata'.
Columnar form that can be
propagated by grafting. Very
rare in Europe. (13)

Picea pungens 'Iseli Foxtail'. This
bizarre form was introduced
by Iseli Nurseries, Boring,
Oregon, U.S.A. (13)

223

Picea pungens 'Iseli Snowkist'. Rather compact growing upright form. Better habit than 'Hoopsii', with the same intense blue color. (13)

Picea pungens 'Kleinod Luusbarg'. Low, broad shrub with grayish green needles. (1)

Picea pungens 'Koster'. The widely known and planted form from Koster. Distributed throughout the world by the firm of Blaauw & Co. formerly in Boskoop, the Netherlands. (61)

Picea pungens 'Lucky Strike'.
New, compact cultivar. Very
young plants bear abundant
cones. (6)

Picea pungens 'Moerheim'. This
cultivar has long, very bright
grayish blue needles, but does
not form a nice plant. Excellent
for cut greenery. (61)

Picea pungens 'Montgomery'.
Slow growing type, often with
a distinct terminal. (71)

225

Picea pungens 'Oldenburg'. An excellent blue spruce discovered in northwestern Germany. (62)

Picea pungens 'Omega'. Does not require staking to develop its very regular habit. (88)

Picea pungens 'St. Mary's Broom'. Originated from a witches'-broom and cultivated in North America. (71)

Picea rubens. Large tree in the Allegheny Mountains. North American Spruce native to the eastern part of the U.S.A.

226

...cea schrenkiana. Tree native to ...ntral Asia and growing to 30 ... The needles are thick and ...ayish green. (13)

Picea sitchensis. Extremely important timber tree in North America. The Sitka Spruce feels less at home in Europe. (30)

...cea sitchensis 'Nana'. Beautiful ...varf spruce. Rarely culti-...ted. Perhaps identical with ...apoose' in England. (61)

Picea sitchensis 'Strypemonde'. Small, compact dwarf. Originated from a witches'-broom on the Estate Strypemonde, the Netherlands. (1)

227

Picea smithiana. Cones.

Picea smithiana. Also known as
P. morinda. This species has the
longest needles of all *Picea*
species. Native to the Himalaya
mountains; not reliably hardy
in cooler climates. (116)

Picea spinulosa. Tall tree; related
to *P. smithiana.* Rare in cultivation. (28)

Pilgerodendron uviferum.
Extremely rare tree from the
Andes mountains; formerly
classified under *Libocedrus.* (116)

Pilgerodendron uviferum. Young
plant. (28)

Pinus albicaulis. Whitebark Pine
on the Tioga Pass. Native to the
western region of North
America.

229

Pinus aristata. Cone with bristles and needles covered with drops of pitch.

Pinus aristata var. *longaeva.* Vigorous tree photographed in Schulman Grove, White Mountains, California.

Pinus armandii. Stemmed co Fine tree with long soft needles. Fairly hardy. (117)

230

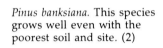

Pinus attenuata. This *Pinus* is also native to California in U.S.A. The cones remain on the tree for many years and release seeds only in extreme heat such as forest fires. Very hardy but yet quite rare. (25)

Pinus banksiana. This species grows well even with the poorest soil and site. (2)

Pinus ayacahuite. Variable species native to the mountains of Mexico. Hardiness depends on the area from which it was obtained. (7)

231

Pinus balfouriana. A beautiful North American species; pictured here in the Onion Valley in the Sierra Nevada. In cultivation also a lovely, little tree.

Pinus balfouriana. Terminal branch of a young plant. (1)

Pinus banksiana 'Compacta'. Although derived from a witches'-broom, grows quite rapidly. (1)

Pinus banksiana 'Tucker's Dwarf'. Also derived from a witches'-broom. Grows much more compactly than the preceding. (63)

Pinus bungeana. Rare species, native to China. Famous for its beautiful bark. (22)

Pinus canariensis. Photographed on Tenerife and native to the Canary Islands. The juvenile needle form remains on this species for many years. Not hardy.

Pinus caribaea. Juvenile leaves sprouting on the trunk. Another species from the Mediterranean region.

233

Pinus cembra. The 'Arve' as this tree is called in Austria and Switzerland. Pictured in Oberwallis, Switzerland.

Pinus cembra. Cone.

Pinus cembra 'Aurea'. A yellow cultivar only attractive during the winter. In the summer all the yellow *Pinus* have a dull, gray quality. (1)

234

Pinus cembra 'Compacta Glauca'. Dense, upright, conical form; developed in Boskoop, the Netherlands about 1950. (61)

Pinus cembroides. Terminal branch of a young tree. This species is native to the south-western region of North America. The seeds (pinons) are edible. (1)

Pinus cembra 'Stricta'. A small tree about 40 years old. Nearly became extinct, but propagated again just in time. (1)

Pinus contorta. Male and female inflorescences. (1)

Pinus contorta. Important forestry tree in its habitat in western North America; planted in enormous quantities for reforestation. (61)

Pinus contorta 'Compacta'.
Weaker growing than the
species but not a dwarf. (1)

Pinus contorta 'Frisian Gold'.
The original sport that originated in a Germany nursery.
The finest yellow cultivar;
retains its color in summer.
(62)

Pinus contorta 'Frisian Gold'.
Young plant grafted from the
sport of the plant shown in the
preceding photo. (1)

Pinus contorta var. *latifolia*.
Photographed in San Bernardino, California. Widespread
in western North America;
valuable timber tree.

Pinus contorta 'Pendula'. Rare; weeping form. (62)

Pinus contorta 'Spaan's Dwarf'. Dwarf form with extremely short needles. More peculiar than nice. (1)

Pinus coulteri. Fairly rare species; very large cones. (41)

Pinus coulteri. The cones are much larger than those of most other species. (1)

Pinus densiflora. Detail of the cone. The inflorescences are closely arranged around the shoots.

Pinus densiflora 'Alice Verkade'. Dwarf form that originated in North America. (13)

Pinus densiflora 'Globosa'. Compact, round dwarf form. (71)

Pinus densiflora 'Oculus-Draconis'. The needles are alternately yellow and green. This feature is clearly visible especially in the growing season. Also called "Dragon eye Pine". (17)

Pinus densiflora 'Pendula'. Small, weeping tree. (80)

Pinus densiflora 'Umbraculifera'. Well-known Japanese semi-dwarf; umbrella-shaped. (1)

Pinus durangensis. A rare species from Mexico. Related to the better known *P. montezumae*.

Pinus flexilis 'Firmament'. Attractive, slender, upright, blue-needled form. Sometimes incorrectly labeled as 'Glauca'. (61)

239

Pinus flexilis 'Glenmore'.
Green-needled, small form;
rare. (71)

Pinus flexilis 'Pendula'.
Weeping form that will gro[w]
flat along the ground unles[s]
staked up. (71)

Pinus flexilis 'Vanderwolfs
Pyramid'. Attractive upright
tree with silvery blue needles.
(1)

Pinus gerardiana. The trunk of
this species is often beautifull[y]
colored.

240

...nus greggii. Detail of the
...nes. Mexican species.

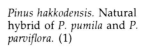

Pinus hakkodensis. Natural
hybrid of *P. pumila* and *P.
parviflora.* (1)

...nus halepensis. Photo-
...aphed in Morocco and native
... most of the Mediterranean
...gion.

Pinus halepensis. Detail of the
stemmed cone.

Pinus jeffreyi. Solitary tree in its North American habitat; Sentinel Dome, Yosemite National Park, California.

Pinus jeffreyi. The annual shoots displaying the typical grayish blue color.

Pinus jeffreyi. A new yellow variegated unnamed cultivar.

242

Pinus koraiensis 'Silveray'. This beautiful form is also marketed as *P. koraiensis* 'Glauca', a misnomer. (1)

...us koraiensis. Cones. (1)

...us kwantungensis. Cone. ...lated to *P. parviflora*.

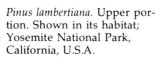

Pinus lambertiana. Upper portion. Shown in its habitat; Yosemite National Park, California, U.S.A.

243

Pinus leucodermis. Branch with cones.

Pinus leucodermis. The Bosnian Pine. This species is always smaller than the related *Pinus nigra*. (1)

Pinus leucodermis 'Aureospicata'. The ends of the needles display a yellow tip. (1)

Pinus leucodermis. Male inflorescence. (1)

Pinus leucodermis 'Satellit'.
Upright habit; needles stand
together as in a shaving brush.
(1)

us leucodermis 'Compact
em'. Excellent slow growing
rm. (1)

us leucodermis 'Schmidtii'.
varf form; the smallest of all
leucodermis cultivars. (62)

Pinus maximartinezii. Very rare
species from Mexico.

245

Pinus monophylla 'Tioga Pass'.
A blue-needled selection from
a wild stand. (13)

Pinus monticola. Cones. Western North American species
widely used for timber.

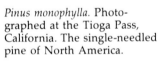

Pinus monophylla. Photographed at the Tioga Pass,
California. The single-needled
pine of North America.

Pinus montezumae. Mexican species with very long, soft needles. (32)

Pinus montezumae. Detail with Mrs. van Hoey Smith.

Pinus monticola 'Ammerland'. New selection with grayish green needles. Young trees have a fairly loose and wild habit. (62)

247

Pinus monticola 'Pendula'.
Young plant of the weeping
form. (17)

Pinus mugo. The Mountain
Pine; found in many forms
in the Alps. This one photographed near Klosters, Switzerland.

Pinus monticola 'Skyline'. Slender, upright cultivar with
bluish gray needles. (1)

Pinus mugo 'Kissen'. Selection
from the variety *pumilio*. (62)

nus mugo 'Frisia'. This form
as found in the dunes near
·rgen, the Netherlands, by
·r. G. Krüssmann. After years
· observation it was intro-
·ıced into cultivation. (62)

Pinus mugo 'Glendale'. Applanated globose form; developed in North America. (62)

Pinus mugo 'Humpy'. One of
the smallest forms of *P. mugo;*
very short needles. (13)

·nus mugo 'Gnom'. Broad,
·ramidal, semi-dwarf;
·veloped in Boskoop, the
·etherlands. (12)

249

Pinus mugo 'Mops'. Widely planted; compact, globose, dwarf form. (1)

Pinus mugo selection Kortmann. Unnamed sport from 'Mops'. (16)

Pinus mugo var. *mughus*. A shrub form found throughout the Alps. Photographed in Yugoslavia together with the creeping variety *P. mugo* var. *pumilio*.

Pinus mugo 'Ophir'. In the winter months this cultivar has an attractive yellow color. (11)

Pinus mugo 'Pal Maleter'. The tips of the needles are yellow; especially conspicuous in the winter. (1)

Pinus mugo var. *pumilio*. The Alpine form on the Parsenn, Switzerland.

251

Pinus mugo var. pumilio 'Esveld Select'. Selected from seedlings; low and broad growing. The plant shown is more than 25 years old. (12)

Pinus mugo 'Rigi'. There is some evidence that this pyramidal form could be classified under P. uncinata. (16)

Pinus mugo 'Trompenburg'. Globose shrub; pictured with an underplanting of Pachysandra terminalis. (1)

Pinus mugo 'Wintergold'. A form that originated in the Netherlands; a nice yellow, especially in winter. (1)

...us muricata. Cones on a tree
...the wild. This species is na-
...e to southwestern U.S.A. to
...rthwestern Mexico.

Pinus nigra. Photographed at
1100 m elevation in Ulu Dag,
Turkey. The habitat of *P. nigra*
extends from Austria into
Turkey.

...us nigra. Old tree in a Swiss
...rden; Mt. Blanc in the back-
...ound. (59)

Pinus nigra 'Aurea'. The young
shoots have golden yellow
needles. (1)

253

Pinus nigra 'Géant de Suisse'.
This cultivar is distinguished
by its very long needles.
Originated with J. P. Meylan,
near Lausanne, Switzerland.
(51)

Pinus nigra 'Columnaris'.
Columnar form, especially
good as a younger tree. (1)

Pinus nigra 'Hornibrookiana'.
Excellent dwarf form for a
somewhat large rock garden.
(1)

Pinus nigra 'Globosa'. Little
known semi-dwarf. (28)

254

Pinus nigra ssp. *laricio.* Better known as *P. nigra* var. *corsicana.* Good timber tree. (70)

Pinus nigra ssp. *pallasiana.* Geographical variety. Photographed in Yugoslavia.

Pinus nigra 'Würstle'. A German introduction that originated as a witches'-broom. Not yet widely available. (62)

Pinus nigra 'Strypemonde'. Shrub form that originated in the Netherlands. Suitable for small gardens. (1)

255

Pinus parviflora 'Adcock's Dwarf'. Excellent dwarf form for the small rock garden. Named for Mr. Adcock, head propagator at Hillier's Nursery, Winchester, U.K.

Pinus parviflora 'Brevifolia'. Small, slow growing tree with very short needles. (28)

Pinus parviflora 'Gimborn's Ideal'. Fairly slender habit; nice bluish gray form. (6)

256

Pinus parviflora 'Glauca'. The needles are somewhat twisted and a nice silvery blue. Very common tree. (1)

Pinus parviflora 'Glauca'. Male inflorescence. (1)

us parviflora 'Glauca'. The nes are formed in fairly large antities even on young trees. (1)

Pinus parviflora 'Glauca'. This cultivar is frequently used for bonsai.

257

Pinus parviflora 'Hagorom
Another Japanese selectic
(63)

Pinus parviflora 'Gyokkasen'.
Japanese selection. (63)

Pinus parviflora 'Schoon's
Bonsai'. Rare dwarf form. (6

Pinus parviflora 'Negishi'. Fairly
slow growing Japanese selection; useful in small gardens.
(6)

Pinus patula. A subtropical, Mexican species distinguished by its long needles.

Pinus parviflora 'Tempelhof'. Fast growing, commonly planted tree. Young trees are often somewhat open and bare. (28)

Pinus peuce. Cones.

Pinus peuce. The Macedonian Pine. Related to *P. cembra.* (33)

Pinus peuce 'Aureovariegata'.
Young shoots bear yellow
needles. (63)

Pinus peuce 'Aurea'. Displays an
attractive yellow, especially in
winter. (62)

Pinus pinaster. The Sea Pi
also known as *P. maritima*
Photographed in the wild
Spain.

Pinus pinaster 'Aberdoniae'.
Discovered and brought into
cultivation near Nice, France.
Hardier than the species. (61)

Pinus pinaster. Old trees in
Cornwall. (112)

Pinus pinea. This tree is characteristic of the Mediterranean
region; pictured here together
with *P. pinaster* in Portugal.

Pinus pinea. Photographed near
Ischia, Italy.

261

Pinus ponderosa. The trunk and the shape of the crown of the tree in the background. A species native to western North America. Photo taken at Willamette State Park, Oregon.

Pinus ponderosa. This tree also feels at home in New Zealand. Photographed at Queenstown.

Pinus ponderosa 'Globosa'. Globose, semi-dwarf.

Pinus ponderosa 'Pendula'. Bizarre, weeping tree. (61)

Pinus ponderosa var. *scopulorum.* The bark is almost black. This natural variety is smaller than the species. (28)

Pinus pringlei. Mexican, tropical species. (3)

Pinus pumila. Male inflorescence. (1)

Pinus pumila 'Chlorocarpa'.
Shrub form that remains low.
Previously classified under *C. cembra*. (27)

Pinus pumila 'Draijer's Dwarf'.
New introduction with a very
promising future. (62)

Pinus pumila 'Glauca'. One of
the best forms of this species;
somewhat variable habit. The
name 'Dwarf Blue' is often
used for this cultivar. (1)

Pinus pumila 'Globe'. Globose
form previously classified
under *P. cembra*. (1)

Pinus pumila 'Saentis'. Upright cultivar; remarkable for a cultivar of *P. pumila*. (17)

nus pumila 'Nana'. This rub-like cultivar is better nown under the incorrect ame *P. cembra* 'Nana'. (1)

Pinus pungens. Cones. This species has sharp needles.

Pinus radiata. Photographed in the original stand on Monterey Peninsula, California. The Monterey Pine, so well-known in America, and widely planted for forestry in Australia, New Zealand, etc., is not hardy in temperate climates.

265

Pinus radiata 'Aurea'. Young tree with golden yellow needles. (28)

Pinus radiata 'Isca'. Old tree in Exeter, Devon with flowering *Prunus*.

Pinus resinosa. Yet unnamed dwarf form derived from a witches'-broom. (1)

Pinus rigida. Native to the east coast of North America. Here with witches'-broom in eastern U.S.A.

Pinus rigida. Suckers on the trunk is characteristic of *P. rigida.*

Pinus roxburghii. In its habitat in Nepal.

Pinus roxburghii. A broad tree; in a park in Kathmandu, Nepal.

267

Pinus × *schwerinii*. One of the few hybrids. The characteristics are intermediate between *P. wallichiana* and *P. strobus*. (21)

Pinus sabiniana. California, U.S.A. species. Not hardy in temperate climates. (41)

Pinus stankewiczii. Cones. Rare Russian species. (32)

Pinus sibirica. Eastern counterpart of *P. cembra*. The needles are much greener and the growth is somewhat faster. (66)

Pinus × *strobiflexilis*. Hybrid between *P. strobus* and *P. flexilis*. The name is possibly not valid; no description has yet been published. (62)

Pinus strobus. The widely planted Weymouth Pine is also used as a rootstock for five-needled cultivars. Unfortunately, this species is rather susceptible to rust. (98)

Pinus strobus 'Alba'. Also known as 'Nivea'. The needles are silvery white. (6)

Pinus strobus 'Aureovariegata'. Yellow-needled form. The name is not validly published. (71)

269

Pinus strobus 'Blue Shag'.
Valuable new cultivar for the
rock garden. (13)

Pinus strobus 'Fastigiata'.
Unattractive as a young tree,
however, later develops a good
columnar form. (6)

Pinus strobus 'Horsford'. Originated from a witches'-broom.
Not widely distributed. (71)

Pinus strobus 'Macopin'. Also originated from a witches'-broom. Bears cones even as a young plant. (38)

Pinus strobus 'Merrimack'. Dwarf form discovered in North America. (71)

Pinus strobus 'Minima'. Dwarf form that has unjustly been long forgotten. (1)

Pinus strobus 'Nana'. More than one clone is sold under this name. 'Umbraculifera' and 'Radiata' are also often offered as 'Nana'. (67)

Pinus strobus 'Pendula'. Attractive, contorted, weeping form. (28)

Pinus strobus 'Prostrata'. Spreading habit. This cultivar is difficult to propagate. (1)

Pinus strobus 'Sea Urchin'. Interesting new dwarf form; suitable for the rock garden. (13)

Pinus strobus 'Torulosa'. The conspicuously twisted needles distinguish this cultivar. (1)

Pinus strobus 'Umbraculifera'. Applanated globose form. Often sold as 'Nana'. (1)

Pinus strobus 'Uncatena'. American novelty; perhaps interesting for other areas as well. (71)

Pinus sylvestris. Typical Scotch Pine in the National Park 'De Hoge Veluwe' near Arnhem, the Netherlands.

273

Pinus sylvestris. Trunk.

Pinus sylvestris 'Alba'. The needles have a white tip; ha[...] the same as the species. (62[...]

Pinus sylvestris 'Argentea'. Shrub form with conspicuous silvery gray needles. (29)

Pinus sylvestris 'Aurea'. The needles are golden yellow in the winter, grayish blue in the summer. Becomes a small tree. (26)

Pinus sylvestris 'Beuvronensis'. d dwarf form that originated France. Grows to about 1 m. 2)

Pinus sylvestris 'Bonna'. Conspicuous blue needles; new cultivar. (17)

Pinus sylvestris 'Fastigiata'. Common, columnar form. Unfortunately has the tendency to become somewhat bare. (63)

Pinus sylvestris 'Fastigiata Draht'. Somewhat thicker form; appears to be an improvement over the preceding cultivar. (61)

275

Pinus sylvestris 'Globosa Viridis'. At the end of each shoot an 'aftershoot' appears, which makes for a somewhat squat appearance. (28)

Pinus sylvestris 'Gold Coin'. The needles are orangy yellow, darker than 'Aurea'. (28)

Pinus sylvestris 'Hillside Creeper'. A true creeping form no higher than 50 cm. (1)

Pinus sylvestris 'Gold Medal'. Summer color is a dull yellow. (28)

Pinus sylvestris 'Lodge Hill'. An irregularly growing dwarf; from a witches'-broom. (75)

Pinus sylvestris 'Moseri'. A yellow-needled form of 'Globosa Viridis'. Although also known incorrectly as *P. nigra* 'Pygmaea' this cultivar has nothing to do with *P. nigra*. (27)

Pinus sylvestris 'Nana'. Large specimen of the true 'Nana'. The much larger growing 'Watereri' is also sold as "Nana." (56)

277

Pinus sylvestris 'Oppdal'. Derived from a witches'-broom and as yet rare on the market. (63)

Pinus sylvestris 'Pixie'. Pyramidal form from a witches'-broom. (75)

Pinus sylvestris 'Repens'. Practically recumbent dwarf form. (71)

Pinus sylvestris 'Saxatilis'. An old but rare creeping form. (71)

Pinus sylvestris 'Spaan's Slow Column'. New, scarce, upright dwarf form. (71)

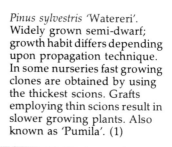

Pinus sylvestris 'Watereri'. Widely grown semi-dwarf; growth habit differs depending upon propagation technique. In some nurseries fast growing clones are obtained by using the thickest scions. Grafts employing thin scions result in slower growing plants. Also known as 'Pumila'. (1)

Pinus tabuliformis. Cone of this Chinese species.

Pinus taeda. Native to southern U.S.A. where it is an important timber tree. (22)

Pinus thunbergii. Cones. The
Japanese Black Pine. Used in
Japan as *P. nigra* is in Europe.
(23)

Pinus thunbergii 'Shiogur(
Compact, globose form;
excellent cultivar.

Pinus thunbergii 'Kotobuki'.
New Japanese cultivar; small,
pyramidal habit and short
needles. (28)

Pinus uncinata. Trunk. Photographed in Graubünden with the typical trees in the background. The nomenclature of this taxon is somewhat confusing. Trees so named are confined to eastern Switzerland and the Tyrol. But the name *P. mugo* var. *rostrata* is also widely used.

Pinus uncinata 'Grüne Welle'. Attractive dwarf form; found as a witches'-broom. (63)

[Pi]nus uncinata 'Leuco-Like'. [N]ew dwarf form that re[se]mbles *P. leucodermis.* Very [in]teresting, but not yet readily [a]vailable. (63)

Pinus uncinata 'Paradekissen'. Exceptionally compact, low, applanated globose form. Still not readily available. (63)

Pinus uncinata var. *rostrata.* Pyramidal form found in nature. Identical to *P. mugo* var. *rostrata.*

Pinus virginiana. Cones. Pictured here in its native habitat Mt. Vernon, U.S.A. Fast growing, usually shrub-like pine; only moderately hardy in temperate climates.

Pinus wallichiana 'Nana'. New, attractive silvery blue, globose form. Fairly rare yet. (62)

Pinus wallichiana. Photographed near Merano, in the Italian Tyrol. The tree with three names: *P. excelsa* and *P. griffithii* are also often used.

Pinus wallichiana. The long cones.

Pinus wallichiana 'Zebrina'. The needles are yellow variegated, especially in winter. (77)

283

Podocarpus acutifolius. One of
the few reasonably hardy
species. The needles are
brownish yellow, especially
in the winter. (113)

Podocarpus alpinus. Slow
growing; suitable for the rock
garden. Reasonably hardy in
temperate climates. (29)

Podocarpus alpinus. Formerly
called *P. lawrencii.* (1)

Podocarpus andinus. Branch of a small tree. Not hardy in temperate zones. (60)

Podocarpus brassii. Detail from a tree in the wild. Native to Australia.

Podocarpus dacrydioides. Photographed at Lake Brunner, New Zealand. Beautiful conifer; unfortunately hardy only in subtropical regions.

Podocarpus falcatus. A row of trees planted for timber production in South Africa.

285

Podocarpus ferrugineus. Fruit.

Podocarpus gracilior. Young plant. (3)

Podocarpus macrophyllus. Detail of branch. Tree native to China. (3)

Podocarpus latifolius. Native to New Zealand. Widely planted in South Africa.

Podocarpus neriifolius. Native to southeast Asia. (22)

Podocarpus nivalis. In the wild in Tangariro National Park, New Zealand. The hardiest of all *Podocarpus* species.

Podocarpus nivalis. The berries. Cultivated plants do not form berries because only one sex is propagated from cuttings.

287

Podocarpus nubigenus. Trunk
with young foliage; photo
taken in Ireland. Native to
Patagonia and Chile. (58)

Podocarpus salignus. Large,
broad tree with leaves that look
a little like those of willow. (58)

Podocarpus spicatus. In its
habitat near Whaiti, New
Zealand with *Dicksonia* (tree
fern).

Podocarpus totara. Enormous trunks shown with the photographer for comparison.

Podocarpus totara. The fruits with the seeds on the outside!

Podocarpus totara 'Aurea'. A slow growing form with yellow leaves. (57)

289

Pseudolarix amabilis. The Golden Larix. This species was also known as *P. kaempferi.* Additionally, for some years this tree was confused with the Japanese Larix, *L. kaempferi,* formerly *L. leptolepis* in nomenclature. Fairly rare in cultivation. (10)

Pseudolarix amabilis. The Golden Larix deserves its name for its fall colors. (1)

Pseudolarix amabilis. Cones. (1)

eudotsuga japonica. Cones. A
ee that does not feel at home
temperate climates.

Pseudotsuga macrocarpa. In the
San Bernardino mountains;
native to southern California,
U.S.A. The cones are larger
than those of the other species.

eudotsuga menziesii 'Blue
onder'. This cultivar has
autiful grayish blue needles.
1)

Pseudotsuga menziesii
'Brevibracteata'. The cones are
much smaller than those of the
species; cone scales are hardly
visible. (61)

Pseudotsuga menziesii. The Douglas Fir is native to North America. Widely planted for timber production.

Pseudotsuga menziesii. Con

Pseudotsuga menziesii 'Elegans'. This tree has irregular branches with grayish blue needles. (61)

Pseudotsuga menziesii 'Fastigiata'. Columnar form; in cultivation for years, yet still relatively rare. (61)

Pseudotsuga menziesii 'Fletcheri'. Good dwarf form with silvery gray needles. Pictured with *Erica carnea* 'King George'. (28)

Pseudotsuga menziesii 'Fretsii'. small tree, not taller than 6–8 , with a compact habit. (23)

Pseudotsuga menziesii 'Fretsii'. Detail of the leaves. (1)

Pseudotsuga menziesii 'Hillside Pride'. Originated from a witches'-broom discovered in North America. (63)

Pseudotsuga menziesii 'Tempelhof Compact'. Broad shrub form; lacks an obvious terminal. (1)

Pseudotsuga menziesii 'Oudemansii'. This tree is smaller than the common Douglas Fir; branches are nearly horizontal. (2)

seudotsuga menziesii 'Varie-
ata'. The needles are silver
ariegated. (1)

Saxegothea conspicua. Native to
Chile; closely resembles *Taxus.*
(21)

ciadopitys verticillata 'Aurea'.
oung plant with golden
ellow needles. Plants growing
nder poor conditions often
ellow, but the quality of color
ffers. (1)

Sciadopitys verticillata 'Green
Star'. A new form; slow
growing, very dark green. (62)

295

Sciadopitys verticillata. The widely grown Umbrella Pine. The leaves are double-needles, i.e., two needles growing together. (1)

Sciadopitys verticillata. Young tree. (61)

Sciadopitys verticillata. Cone. (1)

296

Sequoia sempervirens. The true Redwood from the coastal region of California, U.S.A. Photographed at the beginning of the Avenue of the Giants not far from Crescent City.

Sequoia sempervirens. Cones.

Sequoia sempervirens 'Adpressa'. Small, slow growing cultivar with white needle tips. Irregularly shaped. (1)

297

Sequoia sempervirens 'Prostrata'. Dwarf form, almost recumbent. The needles are shorter and broader than those of the species. (28)

Sequoiadendron giganteum. The Giant Tree of the Sierra Nevada Mountains U.S.A. Fairly hardy in temperate climates. This group is about 50 years old. (68)

Sequoiadendron giganteum. Two trees in the Mariposa Grove in California.

Sequoiadendron giganteum. Many trees in the National Parks of the U.S.A. have been given nicknames; here, the Grizzly Giant.

Sequoiadendron giganteum 'Aurea'. Variegated twigs. (62)

Sequoiadendron giganteum 'Pygmaeum'. Broad pyramidal dwarf form. Rare, but valuable. (1)

Sequoiadendron giganteum 'Glaucum'. Slender, upright cultivar with silvery gray needles. (21)

Sequoiadendron giganteum 'Pendulum'. A bizarre growth habit distinguishes this weeping tree. (27)

299

Taiwania cryptomerioides. A rare tree hardy only in subtropical climates. Resembles *Cryptomeria.* (34)

Taxodium ascendens. Terminal branch of a fairly young tree. The form 'Nutans' can, in fact, hardly be distinguished from the species. (1)

Taxodium ascendens (left) and *Taxodium distichum* (right). The trunks are very different. (1)

Taxodium distichum. Fall colors. Photographed with *Nyssa sylvatica.* (1)

Taxodium distichum. The respiratory knees of *T. distichum;* photo taken at the Estate Queekhoven, Breukelen, ihe Netherlands.

Taxodium distichum. Male inflorescence and cones. (1)

301

Taxodium distichum 'Hursley Park'. A rare dwarf. (1)

Taxodium distichum 'Pendens'. The twigs are slightly pendulous; growth habit is slightly more conical than the species. (1)

Taxodium mucronatum. Old tre in Sydney, Australia. This spe cies is only hardy in subtropical regions.

Taxus baccata. Old trees near church in Kergrist, Brittany, France. In cultivation since antiquity and often planted in cemeteries.

Taxus baccata. Berries. (1)

Taxus baccata. The *Taxus* can be pruned into any conceivable shape. (122)

Taxus baccata 'Adpressa'. The short appressed needles distinguish this cultivar. Berries are similar to those of the species.

Taxus baccata 'Adpressa Aurea'. The needles have yellow edges; otherwise similar to the preceding. (1)

Taxus baccata 'Amersfoort'. Markedly deviant dwarf form discovered in Amersfoort, the Netherlands. Initially thought to be a *Podocarpus*. (1)

Taxus baccata 'Argentea Minor'. Detail of the almost white needles. (1)

Taxus baccata 'Aurea'. In cultivation for years. Habit practically similar to that of the species; however, the needles are bright yellow. (123)

Taxus baccata 'Cappenberg'. Nice columnar form; suitable for narrow hedges. (1)

Taxus baccata 'Cavendishii'. Broad spreading; the needles are stiff and slightly twisted. (51)

Taxus baccata 'Corley's Copper Tip'. The needles are copper colored; originated in the Hatch Nurseries. (1)

Taxus baccata 'Decora' and T. bacc. 'Fastigiata'. 'Decora' is a fine dwarf form, but is fairly rare. (124)

Taxus baccata 'Dovastoniana'. very well-known tree of aberrant habit. Cuttings taken from side shoots almost nev develop a terminal. (21)

Taxus baccata 'Erecta Aureovariegata'. The needles are yellow-edged. (17)

Taxus baccata 'Dovastonii Aurea'. The same habit as the preceding, but the needles have a yellow edge. (61)

Taxus baccata 'Fastigiata'. The well-known Irish Taxus; a very old specimen in Ireland. (124)

Taxus baccata 'Fastigiata Aurea'. The yellow-needled form can become almost as tall as the green-needled form. (126)

Taxus baccata 'Fastigiata Robusta'. Cigar-shaped, very dense and very hardy cultivar. (1)

Taxus baccata 'Flushing'. Suitable for hedges. (17)

Taxus baccata 'Giraldii'. Old form that has fallen into oblivion. (2)

Taxus baccata 'Goudelsje'. Fresh yellow shrub form; remains small. (2)

Taxus baccata 'Ingeborg Nellemann'. A yellow needl shrub form which deserves greater distribution. (61)

Taxus baccata 'Graciosa'. Shrub-like tree; rarely cultivated. (1)

Taxus baccata 'Lutea'. One of the
few *Taxus* forms with bright
yellow berries.

Taxus baccata 'Jacksonii'. Low,
spreading shrub with yellow
needles. (21)

Taxus baccata 'Melford'. One of
the numerous columnar forms;
very hardy. (61)

Taxus baccata 'Newport'. A rare,
dense columnar form. (17)

Taxus baccata 'Nutans'. Dwarf form; rarely becomes more than 50 cm tall. (2)

Taxus baccata 'Parvula'. A broa form with short needles. (29

Taxus baccata 'Procumbens'. Very broad growing form; turns a bronze color in winter. (17)

Taxus baccata 'Repandens'. Widely grown, flat growing cultivar; well suited for public plantings. (61)

Taxus baccata 'Repandens Aurea'. Resembles the well-known 'Summergold'. Plants propagated from sideshoots of 'Dovastonii Aurea', are frequently sold under this name. (1)

Taxus baccata 'Schwarzgrün'. German introduction with very dark green needles. (61)

Taxus baccata 'Semperaurea'. Bright golden yellow needles adorn this shrub-like cultivar. (4)

311

Taxus baccata 'Standishii'. Berries.

Taxus baccata 'Standishii'. Slow growing, dense and compact; the nicest yellow-needled, columnar form. (107)

Taxus baccata 'Summergold'. Shrub-like cultivar bearing handsome golden yellow needles, especially in the summer. (86)

Taxus baccata 'Stricta Viridis'. Beautiful, columnar form, with long, broad needles. (61)

Taxus baccata 'Washingtonii'.
Broad, upright, shrub form; the
needles are not true yellow,
but more greenish yellow. (1)

Taxus baccata 'Thomsen'. Broad,
columnar form; not yet widely
distributed. (61)

Taxus cuspidata. Berries. This
species is native to Japan; little
planted in Europe but widely
planted in the United States. (1)

Taxus baccata 'Weeping Girl'.
Not a very appropriate name
for this globose form. (17)

Taxus cuspidata 'Capitata
Aurea'. Shrub form. (2)

Taxus cuspidata 'Luteobaccata'.
The yellow-berried form of
Japanese *Taxus*.

Taxus media 'Hicksii'. Widely
planted as a hedge. The author
has decided to show only one
of these forms; the slight differences are not well illustrated in photographs. (83)

Taxus media 'Nidiformis'. Broad
growing shrub form; the center
of the plant forms a nest. (17)

Taxus media 'Sentinalis'. The narrowest columnar form of all the *T. media* selections. (17)

Taxus media 'Thayerae'. Very hardy, somewhat untidy shrub form. Suitable for large beds in public plantings. (28)

Taxus media 'Wellesleyana'. Coarse shrub form; rather rare. (2)

Taxus wallichiana. Tree in its natural habitat of Nepal. There it develops into a fairly tall tree.

Taxus wallichiana. The trunk has a beautiful color.

Taxus wallichiana var. *chinensis.* Detail of needles. (29)

316

Tetraclinis articulata. This rare conifer is native to north Africa with an isolated habitat in southern Spain. It is a valuable tree for dry, warm climates.

Tetraclinis articulata. Cones.

Thuja koraiensis. Detail of branch and the silver colored underside. This Korean *Thuja* almost always remains shrub-like, rarely growing into a small tree. (1)

Thuja occidentalis. Cones. The western Tree of Life. A universally known species that is widely planted, often for hedges. Somewhat sensitive to sea wind, and therefore more commonly used in continental climates.

Thuja occidentalis 'Argentea'. The plant presents a nearly white appearance; scales at the tips of the twiglets are practically white. (61)

Thuja occidentalis 'Beaufort'. A mutation of the preceding cultivar, which is broader and lower. (61)

Thuja occidentalis 'Cristata Aurea'. Slender, dense dwarf form with twisted twiglets. (61)

Thuja occidentalis 'Danica'. Dwarf form; often used for containers and in cemetery plantings. (61)

Thuja occidentalis 'Douglasii
Aurea'. A broad, good yellow,
conical form; rarely planted.
(1)

Thuja occidentalis 'Elegantissima'. Widely cultivated in
the past, but little used today.
(61)

Thuja occidentalis 'Europe
Gold'. Dark golden yellow
columnar form, selected in the
Netherlands. Photograph by
the producer of this cultivar.
(127)

Thuja occidentalis 'Fehnsilber'.
A variegated form selected in
northern Germany. (61)

319

Thuja occidentalis 'Filiformis'. Compact, conical form with thread-like twigs. (61)

Thuja occidentalis 'Giganteoides'. Fast growing tree discovered in Denmark about 1935 in a seedling lot. (21)

Thuja occidentalis 'Globosa'. An old, globose form which still deserves a place in gardens. (128)

Thuja occidentalis 'Golden Globe'. Fine, yellow, globose form; keeps its color well even in winter. (14)

Thuja occidentalis 'Hetz Midget'. Extremely slow growing; globose form, somewhat irregularly shaped. (1)

Thuja occidentalis 'Holmstrup'. Attractive, fresh green, thick columnar form; often planted. (28)

Thuja occidentalis 'Holmstrup Yellow'. Mutation of the preceding. (1)

Thuja occidentalis 'Little Champion'. Globose form that is fairly tolerant of snow load; most *Thuja* globose forms are not. (61)

Thuja occidentalis 'Little Gem'. An applanated, slightly irregular dwarf form. (61)

Thuja occidentalis 'Lutea'. A yellow *Thuja* seldom cultivated as the new 'Sunkist' is much better. (1)

Thuja occidentalis 'Malonyana'. Original specimens. Attractive columnar form developed in Czechoslovakia. This beautiful form is seldom cultivated, but deserves more attention. (82)

Thuja occidentalis 'Meckii'. Slow growing dwarf. (61)

Thuja occidentalis 'Meineke's Zwerg'. Slow growing dwarf form; reaches a height of about 60 cm in 15 years. (61)

Thuja occidentalis 'Menhir'. Novelty, with an original name. (129)

323

Thuja occidentalis 'Milleri'. In a rose garden. Irregular, broad, dwarf form. (1)

Thuja occidentalis 'Ohlendorffii'. Retains its juvenile form. Thread-like twigs; very attractive as young plant, but somewhat untidy when older. (1)

Thuja occidentalis 'Pendula'. Small, weeping tree, usually with very irregular habit. (28)

Thuja occidentalis 'Perk Vlaanderen'. Detail of the yellow variegated twigs. (1)

Thuja occidentalis 'Recurva Nana'. Long cultivated, but now somewhat overlooked shrub form. (16)

Thuja occidentalis 'Pyramidalis Compacta'. Widely planted columnar form; resembles 'Columna'. Also commonly called 'Fastigiata'. (61)

Thuja occidentalis 'Rosenthalii'. One of the best columnar forms; fairly slow growing. (2)

Thuja occidentalis 'Rheingold'. A
very large specimen. Widley cultivated
emi-dwarf with an attractive yellow
olor. When bought young with juvenile
eedles, it soon reverts to the above
nature form, also known as *T.o.* 'Elwangeriana
urea'. (113)

Thuja occidentalis 'Smaragd'. Known as 'Emerald' in England and as 'Emeraude' in France; however, 'Smaragd' is the correct name. At present an important cultivar, cultivated and sold in large quantities. (4)

Thuja occidentalis 'Spiralis'. Spirally twisted twigs distinguish this old-time tree. (28

Thuja occidentalis 'Steuberi'. The twigs are yellow, while the foliage is green. (61)

Thuja occidentalis 'Sunkist'. Exceptionally good, attractive, yellow form that is now often planted. (1)

Thuja occidentalis 'Tiny Tim'.
Superb dwarf form; well suited
for the rock garden. (1)

Thuja occidentalis
'Trompenburg'. Fairly broad,
upright, yellow cultivar. (1)

Thuja occidentalis
'Umbraculifera'. Applanated
globose form, much broader
than high. (61)

Thuja occidentalis 'Wansdyke
Silver'. Detail of this new
variegated dwarf form.

Thuja occidentalis 'Wareana Lutescens'. Columnar form; somewhat fallen out of style. (61)

Thuja occidentalis 'Waxen'. Loose, graceful, small tree developed in the Arnold Arboretum, Cambridge, Mass., U.S.A. (2)

Thuja orientalis 'Athrotaxoides'. A broad, slow growing, conical form. Rarely planted. (34)

328

Thuja orientalis. The eastern Tree of Life. Much less common than *T. occidentalis* and slightly less hardy. (5)

Thuja orientalis 'Aurea Nana'.
A nice, golden yellow, dwarf
form. Also sold under the
incorrect name 'Bergmannii'.
(1)

Thuja orientalis 'Blue Cone'.
New, bluish green, columnar
form. (17)

Thuja orientalis 'Blijdenstein'.
Very broad spreading; original
plant is not as high as it is
broad. (3)

329

Thuja orientalis 'Elegantissima'.
This form is very frequently
planted in France and Italy. (1)

Thuja orientalis 'Filiformis
Erecta'. Dwarf form; fairly stiff,
upright habit. (40)

Thuja orientalis 'Filiformis
Pendula'. Weeping form of the
former. (89)

Thuja orientalis 'Juniperoides'.
The winter color is striking. (1)

Thuja orientalis 'Meldensis'. An ovate habit, which is uncommon in *Thuja*. (28)

Thuja orientalis 'Minima'. Dwarf form. Plants sold under the name 'Minima Glauca' are identical to this cultivar. (1)

Thuja orientalis 'Rosedalis'. Dwarf form with needlelike leaves. (38)

Thuja orientalis 'Pyramidalis Aurea'. Tall, columnar form; especially common in Italy. (1)

Thuja orientalis 'Sanderi'. Also in cultivation as *Chamaecyparis obtusa* 'Sanderi'. (1)

Thuja orientalis 'Sanderi'. Winter color. (1)

Thuja orientalis 'Tetragona'. Dwarf form; resembles 'Filiformis Erecta', but of somewhat more regular habit. (1)

Thuja orientalis 'Wang's Green'. A small, compact, globose form from a chance seedling. (15)

Thuja plicata 'Atrovirens'.
Cultivated in large quantities
for hedges in France and Italy.
Also makes a very nice solitary
tree. (125)

Thuja plicata. This species also
grows large in cultivation. (1)

Thuja plicata. The lowest
branches root where they
touch the ground and form
new trees. (1)

Thuja plicata 'Cuprea'. Yellow scales. (1)

Thuja plicata 'Gracilis Aurea'. Graceful little tree with slightly pendulous twigs. (1)

Thuja plicata 'Hillieri'. Good dark green, very dense, globose form. (28)

334

Thuja plicata 'Pumila'. One of the few dwarf forms of this large tree. (1)

Thuja plicata 'Rogersii'. Conical dwarf form that is yellow in the summer and bronze in winter. (1)

Thuja plicata 'Stoneham Gold'. Fine, gold colored, conical form; grows fairly slow. (1)

Thuja plicata 'Zebrina'. Large tree; dotted with golden yellow twiglets.

335

Thuja plicata 'Zebrina Extra Gold'. Detail. Intense yellow. (1)

Thuja standishii. Very hardy small tree; often somewhat irregular habit. (85)

Thujopsis dolabrata. This species forms a fast growing continuous terminal only when older. (109)

Thujopsis dolabrata. Branch with cones.

Thujopsis dolabrata 'Altissima'.
This cultivar grows taller than
the species and has a looser
habit. (3)

Thujopsis dolabrata 'Cristata'.
The twiglets are twisted at the
tip. (100)

Thujopsis dolabrata 'Aurescens'.
Good soft yellow; remains low.
(38)

Thujopsis dolabrata 'Nana'. This superb conifer deserves much more attention. (1)

Torreya californica. Male inflorescence. This fairly rare tree i native to California, U.S.A. Resembles *Cephalotaxus* but has sharp needles.

Thujopsis dolabrata 'Variegata'. Shorter than the species; covered with white twiglets. (61)

Torreya californica. Fruits.

Torreya nucifera. Old tree. This species is native to Japan.

Torreya nucifera. Fruits. (1)

Torreya nucifera 'Prostrata'. A creeping form; rare in cultivation. (124)

339

Torreya nucifera 'Variegata'.
Needles are white variegated.
(47)

340

Tsuga canadensis. The Hemlock.
In the past skis were made
from the wood. (1)

Tsuga canadensis 'Albospica'.
Slow growing, with many
white needles. (61)

Tsuga canadensis 'Ammerland'. An excellent new German selection. (61)

Tsuga canadensis 'Brandley'. A beautiful, spreading plant; American introduction. (13)

Tsuga canadensis 'Cole'. Resembles the well-known 'Pendula' but stays lower. (1)

Tsuga canadensis 'Compacta'. Flat, globose form; resembles 'Jeddeloh'. (28)

Tsuga canadensis 'Fantana'.
Irregular shrub form.

Tsuga canadensis 'Everitt
Golden'. Upright yellow-
needled cultivar. Sometimes
sold as 'Gracilis Aurea'. (1)

Tsuga canadensis 'Fremdii'.
Rare, broad, conical cultivar.
(2)

342

Tsuga canadensis 'Gracilis'.
Applanated globose form;
slow growing. (1)

Tsuga canadensis 'Horstmann'.
From a witches'-broom. (63)

Tsuga canadensis 'Jeddeloh'.
Widely cultivated nest-shaped
dwarf form. The center of the
plant is always slightly
depressed. (4)

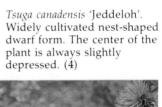

343

Tsuga canadensis 'Lutea'. With beautiful yellow needles. (28)

Tsuga canadensis 'Minima'. The twiglets of this mini-Hemlock are barely longer than 2 cm. (61)

Tsuga canadensis 'Verkade's Recurved'. A beautiful dwarf form with twisted needles. (13)

Tsuga canadensis 'Parvifolia'. Detail of the needles. Shrub form with extremely short, small needles. (1)

344

Tsuga canadensis 'Pendula'. Well-known weeping form with various growth habits; here as a small, weeping tree. (3)

Tsuga canadensis 'Prostrata'. A dwarf form of 'Pendula'. (1)

Tsuga canadensis 'Watnong Star'. Compact, globose form. (101)

Tsuga caroliniana. Tree to 15 m; fairly rare in gardens and parks.

345

Tsuga caroliniana 'La Bar's Weeping'. Weeping form, often practically creeping. (71)

Tsuga chinensis. The Chinese *Tsuga,* related to the *T. dumosa,* is native to the Himalayas. (114)

Tsuga diversifolia. Detail of the inflorescence. A Japanese species with very dark green needles.

Tsuga dumosa. In Kilbogget Garden, Dublin, Ireland. Native to Nepal and the Himalayas.

Tsuga dumosa. Cones.

Tsuga heterophylla. Native to the coniferous forests of western North America. A very valuable forestry tree. (2)

Tsuga heterophylla. Cones.

347

Tsuga heterophylla 'Conica'. Semi-dwarf form that is unjustifiably scarce. (2)

Tsuga × *jeffreyi*. One of the few hybrids in this genus. (2)

Tsuga × *jeffreyi*. Detail.

Tsuga mertensiana 'Blue Star'.
This cultivar has beautiful
grayish blue needles. Unfortunately, it is very difficult to
propagate. (2)

Tsuga mertensiana 'Nana'.
Very broad, conical form with
grayish blue needles. (9)

Tsuga sieboldii. Cones.

Tsuga sieboldii 'Nana'. Small globose form; very attractive, but rare. (1)

Widdringtonia cupressoides. In the wild in south Africa.

Widdringtonia cupressoides. Cones.

Widdringtonia schwarzii. Young plant. (75)

APPENDICES

Hardiness Zones and the British Isles by Kenneth Beckett

Very few of the trees, shrubs and other garden plants cultivated in Britain are native to the British Isles. Over the centuries they have been introduced from all over the world, though especially from cool and warm temperate climates. How well they thrive in the British Isles largely depends on the climate they evolved in.

Although all plants are closely adapted to the climate of the region in which they occur wild, few have rigid requirements of heat and cold. There are other factors that decide whether a plant will thrive, e.g. soil type and amount of rainfall, but these will be mentioned later; temperature is of primary importance.

The British Isles has an equable oceanic climate which is seldom very cold, hot or dry. As a result, a wide range of the world's plants can be grown outside providing they are sited intelligently. Undoubtedly, some of these plants would prefer more summer sun or a more definite cold winter rest, but their innate adaptability is catered for in the vagaries of our climate. There is, however, a point at which a plant's tolerance ceases. Low temperature is the most important of these tolerances. If a plant cannot survive an average winter outside it is said to be tender. If a plant survives average winters but not the exceptionally hard one it is said to be half-hardy. These terms are, of course, relevant only to the area in which one lives.

Large continental land masses, e.g. North America and Central Europe, have climates that get progressively colder winters as one proceeds northwards and further inland from the sea. North America provides a familiar example, the extreme south being almost tropical, the far north arctic. In the 1930s, the United States Department of Agriculture divided the USA into 7 hardiness zones based upon an average of the absolute minimum temperatures over a period of 20 years. Later, the system was revised and refined and 10 zones recognized (zone 1 is arctic, zone 10 tropical). More recently this Hardiness Zone system has been extended to Europe, including the British Isles. Gardeners in the United States and Canada soon took advantage of the hardiness zone concept and over the years, largely by trial and error, most trees and shrubs and many other plants have been assessed and given zone ratings. Nevertheless, this system, though useful, can only be considered to give approximate hardiness ratings, especially when applied to the British Isles.

Sitting as it does on the eastern edge of the North Atlantic Ocean, the British Isles occupies a unique position. Although its total length, about 650 miles (Cornwall to Orkney), lies within latitudes 50° to 60° N, it falls into zone 8! Moved into the same latitudes in North America, it would lie entirely north of the Canadian border with the tip of Cornwall level with Winnipeg (zone 2–3). Even the eastern coastal region of Canada at these latitudes is no warmer than zones 3–4. Because of the influence of the Gulf Stream the British Isles enjoys a remarkably uniform climate. Such temperature gradients as these are run east to west rather than south to north.

It is a characteristic of temperate oceanic climates to have milder winters and cooler summers than equivalent continental ones and because of their northerly position this is even more marked in the British Isles. For this reason, a number of trees and shrubs which thrive in zone 8 in USA

fail to do so well in Britain e.g., *Albizia julibrissin, Lagerstroemia indica,* etc. Such plants may live but fail to bloom, or get cut back severely by the British winters. The factor is primarily lack of summer sun rather than absolute cold.

This lack of summer warmth brings us to the several important ancillary factors which affect a plant's hardiness. Apart from lack of damaging low temperatures a plant needs the right kind of soil, adequate rainfall and humidity, plus sufficient light intensity and warmth. As with low temperature most plants have fairly wide tolerances, though there are noteworthy exceptions. Most members of the Ericaceae, especially *Rhododendron* and allied genera, must have an acid soil or they will die however perfect the climate. For plants near the limits of their cold tolerance, shelter is essential. Protection from freezing winds is particularly important. This can be provided by planting in the lee of hedges, fences and walls or among trees with a fairly high canopy. Individual plants can also be protected by matting or plastic sheeting or the bases can be earthed up or mounded around with peat, coarse sand or weathered boiler ash. A thick layer of snow also provides insulation against wind and radiation frost! Plenty of sunshine promotes firm, ripened growth with good food reserves, notably a high sugar content in the cell sap which then takes longer to freeze. If the summer is poor a partial remedy is to apply sulphate of potash (at 10g/per square metre) in late summer. This will boost the amount of sugars and starches in the plant. Half-hardy plants will stand having their tissues moderately frozen providing the thawing-out is gradual. For this reason it is best to grow them in a sheltered site which does not get the first rays of the morning sun. This is especially relevant for species with tender young leaves or early flowers, e.g. *Cercidiphyllum, Camellia* and *Magnolia*.

Zone 9 in the USA is warm-temperate to sub-tropical with hot summers. In the British Isles it tends to have even cooler summers than zone 8, and as a result very few truly sub-tropical plants can be grown in Britain. Most of the plants in the famous so-called, sub-tropical gardens, e.g. Tresco, Logan, Inverewe, etc., are of warm-temperate origin. For the reasons set down above, in Britain, if in doubt, it is best to consider zone 8 as zone 7 and zone 9 as zone 8 for plants of unreliable hardiness.

With the extensive introduction of foreign plant material, the question of hardiness and the classification of material in climatic zones has been much discussed among dendrologists. The difficulty lies in the fact that the hardiness of a particular plant or species is variable and not absolute. In most cases, the critical factor in a plant's ability to survive is the minimum average winter temperature. But the influence of many other factors affecting the plant cannot be underestimated; i.e. summer heat, temperature range, annual rainfall and its distribution, snowfall, winter sun intensity, wind and various soil factors.

It should be noted that the winter hardiness ratings can serve only as rough guidelines. The local climate within a particular zone may vary considerably due to altitude, slopes, valleys, cities, bodies of water, windbreaks, etc. It should also be noted that the absolute minimum temperature recorded for a particular period might lie as much as 11°C lower than the average minimum. For the most successful results, one should use plants with the best tolerance of late frosts and the best adaptation to the growing season of the microclimate.

353

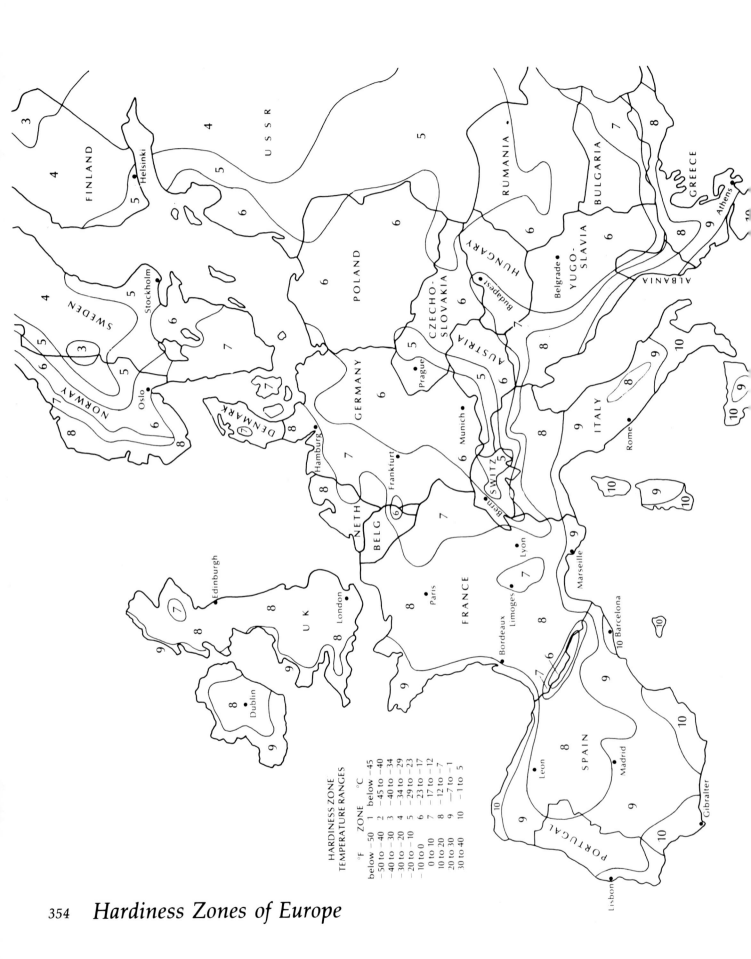

HARDINESS ZONE
TEMPERATURE RANGES

°F	ZONE	°C
below −50	1	below −45
−50 to −40	2	−45 to −40
−40 to −30	3	−40 to −34
−30 to −20	4	−34 to −29
−20 to −10	5	−29 to −23
−10 to 0	6	−23 to −17
0 to 10	7	−17 to −12
10 to 20	8	−12 to −7
20 to 30	9	−7 to −1
30 to 40	10	−1 to 5

354 *Hardiness Zones of Europe*

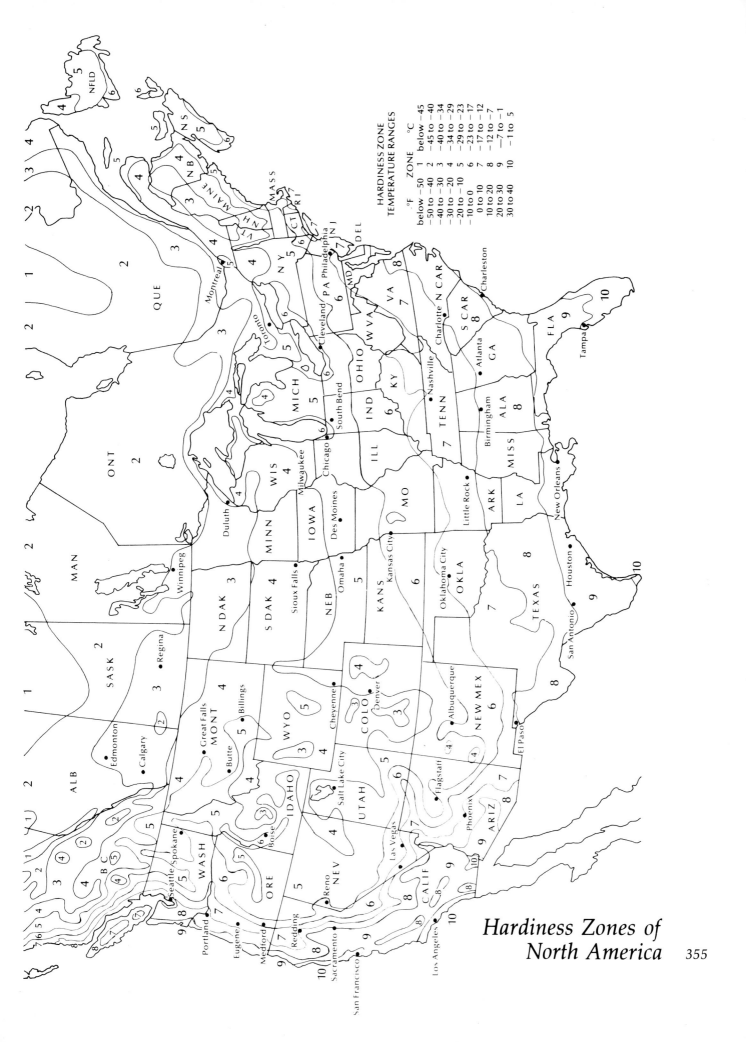

HARDINESS ZONE
TEMPERATURE RANGES

°F		ZONE		°C
below −50		1		below −45
−50 to −40		2		−45 to −40
−40 to −30		3		−40 to −34
−30 to −20		4		−34 to −29
−20 to −10		5		−29 to −23
−10 to 0		6		−23 to −17
0 to 10		7		−17 to −12
10 to 20		8		−12 to −7
20 to 30		9		−7 to −1
30 to 40		10		−1 to 5

Hardiness Zones of North America   355

Hardiness Zones of China

SOVIET UNION

Mongolia

Heilongjiang

Jilin

Xinjiang

Liaoning

Inner Mongolia

KOREA

Gansu
Kansu

Hebei

−4° C

PEOPLE'S REPUBLIC OF CHINA

Ningxia

Shanxi

Shandong
Shantung

0° C

JAPAN

Qinghai

Shaanxi
Shenshi

Jiangsu
Kiangsi

Tibet

Henan

Anhui

4° C

NEPAL

Hubei
Hupeh

Zhejiang
Chekiang

8° C

SIKKIM

Sichuan
Szechuan

BHUTAN

Hunan

Jiangxi

Fujian
Fukien

12° C

INDIA

ASSAM

Guizhou
Kweichow

Tropic of Cancer

BANGLADESH

Yunnan

Guangxi
Kwangshi

Guangdong
Kwangtung

TAIWAN

BURMA

VIETNAM

LAOS

HAINAN

PHILIPPINES

THAILAND

CAMBODIA

HARDINESS ZONE
TEMPERATURE RANGES

°F	ZONE	°C
below −50	1	below −45
−50 to −40	2	−45 to −40
−40 to −30	3	−40 to −34
−30 to −20	4	−34 to −29
−20 to −10	5	−29 to −23
−10 to 0	6	−23 to −17
0 to 10	7	−17 to −12
10 to 20	8	−12 to −7
20 to 30	9	−7 to −1
30 to 40	10	−1 to 5

N. BORNEO

INDONESIA

MALAYSIA

MALAYSIA

Cone Drawings

The cone drawings are included according to *Unsere Freiland-Nadelhölze* by Ernst Graf Silva Tarouca and Camillo Schneider (First edition, 1913). These drawings compiled by J.R.P. Van Hoey mith and completed by Inez de Maaré. In this index to the drawings, numbers following the entries indicate size of the drawings relative to the size of actual cones.

ABIES

1.	alba	2/3
2.	amabilis	1/2
3.	balsamea	1
4.	bracteata	1/2
5.	cephalonica	2/3
6.	cilicica	1/2
7.	concolor	1
8.	delavayi	2/3
9.	fargesii	2/3
10.	firma	2/3
11.	grandis	1
12.	homolepis	2/3
13.	lasiocarpa	1
14.	lasiocarpa v. arizonica	1
15.	magnifica	1/2
16.	mariesii	1
17.	nordmanniana	2/3
18.	numidica	2/3
19.	pindrow	2/3
20.	pinsapo	2/3
21.	procera	1/2
22.	religiosa	2/3
23.	sachalinensis	1
24.	sibirica	1
25.	spectabilis	1/2
26.	squamata	2/3
27.	veitchii	1

ARAUCARIA

28.	araucana	2/3

CEDRUS

29.	atlantica	2/3
30.	deodara	2/3
31.	libani	2/3

CUPRESSUS

32.	macrocarpa	1

KETELEERIA

33.	davidiana	2/3
34.	evelyniana	2/3

LARIX

35.	gmelinii v. principis-ruprechtii	1
36.	griffithiana	1
37.	lyallii	1
38.	occidentalis	1
39.	potaninii	1

PICEA

40.	abies	1
41.	alcoquiana	1
42.	brachytyla v. complanata	2/3
43.	breweriana	1
44.	engelmannii	1
45.	glauca	1
46.	glehnii	1
47.	jezoensis	1
48.	jezoensis v. hondoensis	1
49.	mariana	1
50.	montigena	1

PICEA

51.	neoveitchii	2/3
52.	obovata	1
53.	omorika	1
54.	orientalis	1
55.	polita	1
56.	pungens	1
57.	rubens	1
58.	schrenkiana	1
59.	sitchensis	1
60.	smithiana	1
61.	spinulosa	1
62.	wilsonii	1

PINUS

63.	aristata	2/3
64.	armandii	1/2
65.	attenuata	1
66.	banksiana	1
67.	brutia	1
68.	bungeana	1
69.	canariensis	2/3
70.	cembra	1
71.	cembroides v. edulis	1
72.	contorta	1
73.	coulteri	1/2
74.	densiflora	1
75.	echinata	1
76.	flexilis	1
77.	gerardiana	2/3
78.	halepensis	1/2
79.	jeffreyi	1/2
80.	koraiensis	1/2
81.	lambertiana	1/3
82.	leucodermis	1
83.	monophylla	1
84.	montezumae v. hartwegii	1
85.	monticola	1/2
86.	mugo	1
87.	muricata	1
88.	nigra ssp. nigra	1
89.	palustris	1/2
90.	parviflora	1
91.	patula	1
92.	peuce	2/3
93.	pinaster	2/3
94.	pinea	2/3
95.	ponderosa	2/3
96.	pumila	1
97.	pungens	1
98.	radiata	2/3
99.	resinosa	1
100.	rigida	1
101.	sabiniana	2/3
102.	strobus	2/3
103.	sylvestris	1
104.	taeda	2/3
105.	teocote	2/3
106.	thunbergii	1
107.	torreyana	1/2
108.	virginiana	1
109.	wallichiana	1/2
110.	yunnanensis	2/3

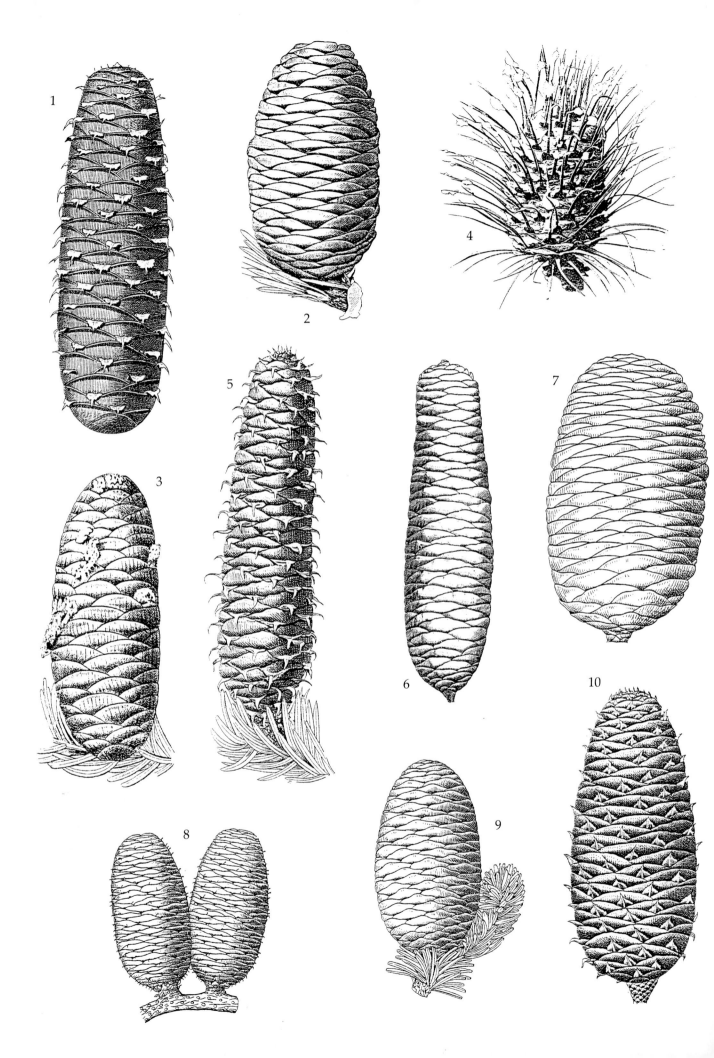

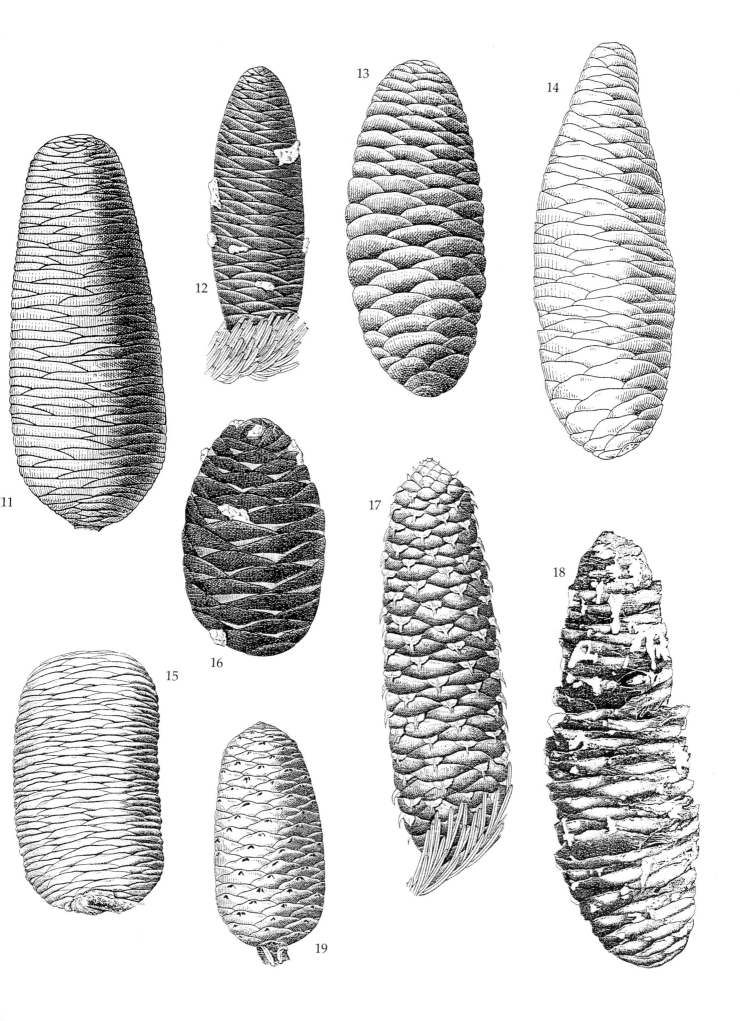

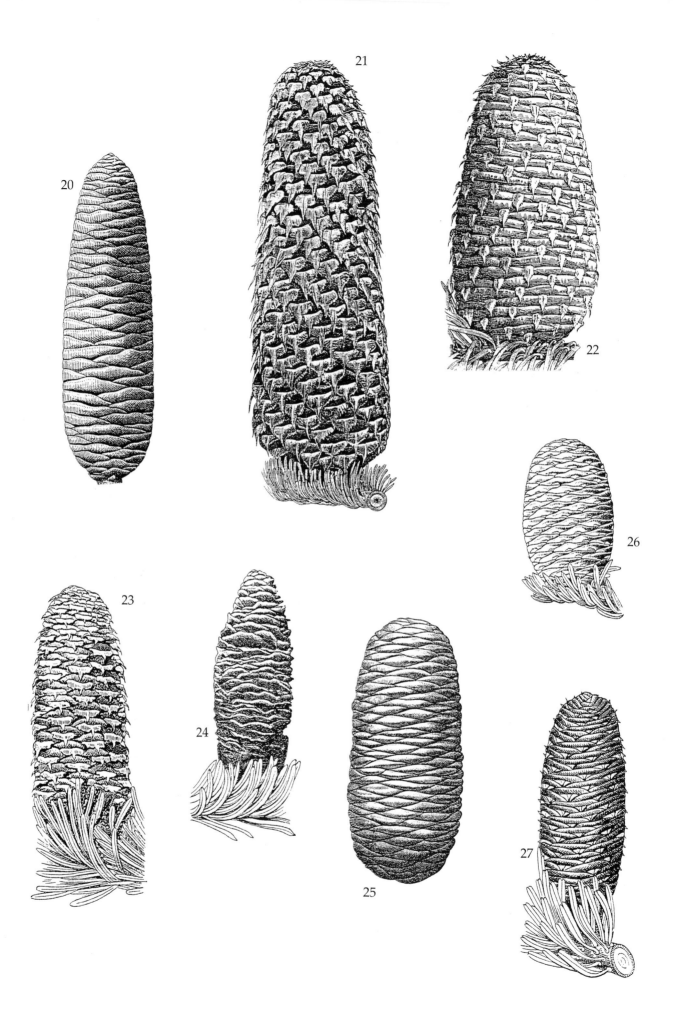

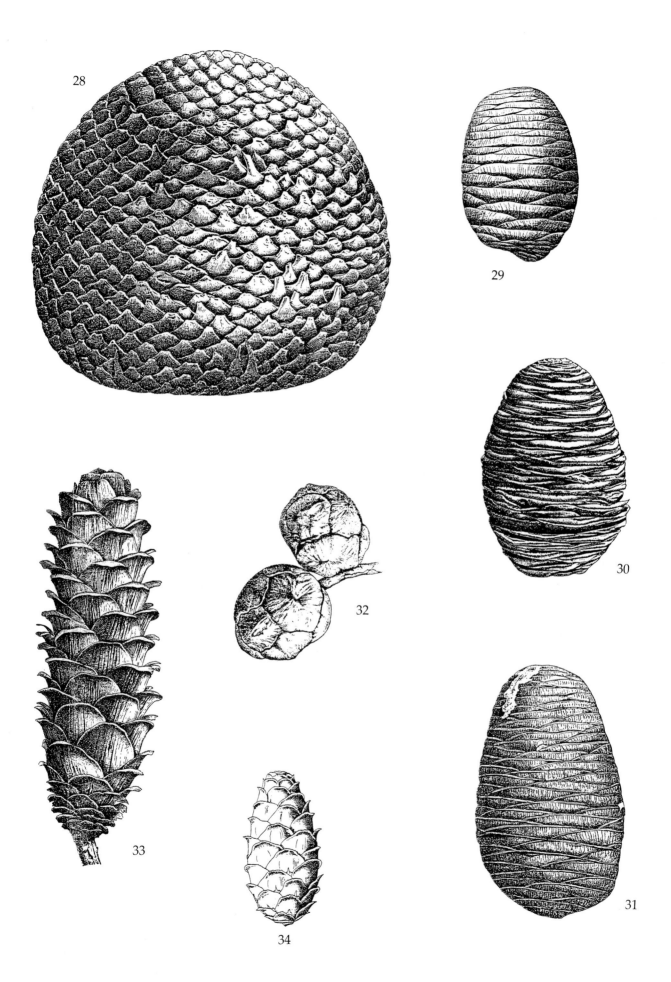

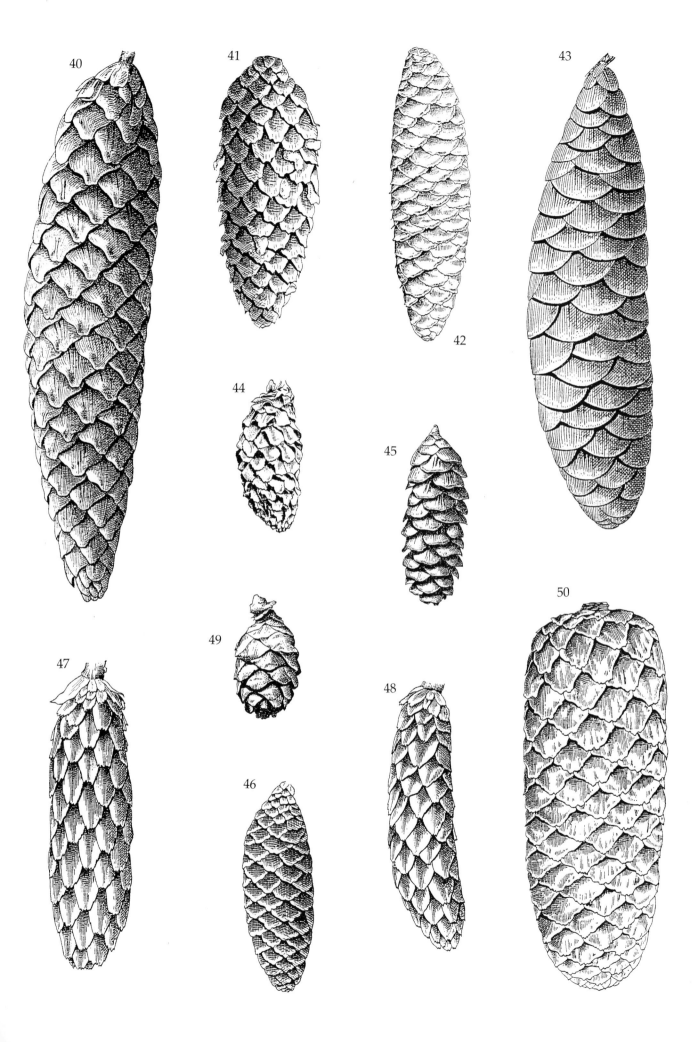

82

83

84

85

87

88

89

86

90

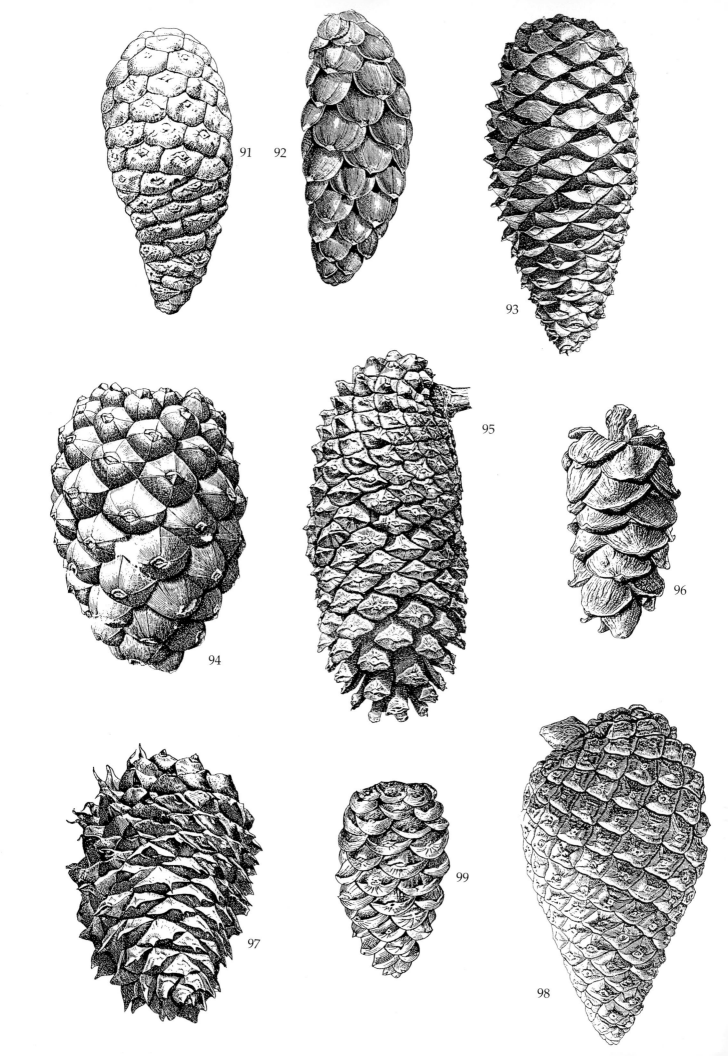

91   92

93

95

94

96

97

99

98

100

101

102

103

104

105

106

107

108

109

110